PARIS WALKS

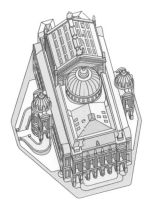

PARIS WALKS

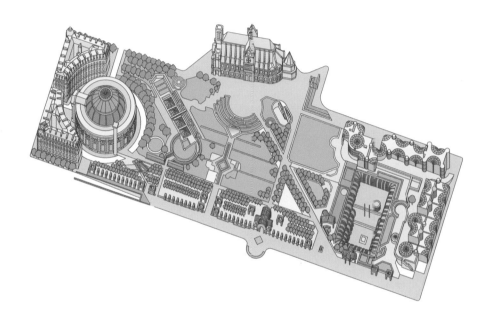

Second Edition

Fiona Duncan & Leonie Glass

DUNCAN PETERSEN

INSIDERS' GUIDE®

GUILFORD, CONNECTICUT
AN IMPRINT OF THE GLOBE PEQUOT PRESS

Copyright © Fiona Duncan and Leonie Glass
Copyright © 2001, 2006 Duncan Petersen Publishing Ltd

This updated edition published 2006 by:
Duncan Petersen Publishing Limited
C7, Old Imperial Laundry
Warriner Gardens, London SW11 4XW
United Kingdom

Published in the USA by:
The Globe Pequot Press, LLC
P.O. Box 480
Guilford, CT 06437
Insiders' Guide is a registered trademark of The Globe Pequot Press.

Sales representation and distribution in the U.K. and Ireland by Portfolio Books Limited
Unit 5, Perivale Industrial Park
Horsenden Lane South
Greenford UB6 7RL
Tel: 0208 997 9000

UK ISBN-13: 978-1-903301-45-6
UK ISBN-10: 1-903301-45-9
North America ISBN-13: 978-0-7627-4160-1
North America ISBN-10: 0-7627-4160-0

A CIP catalogue record for this book is available from the British Library.
Library of Congress Cataloging-in-Publication Data is available.
Conceived, designed and produced by
Duncan Petersen Publishing Ltd

Editorial Director Andrew Duncan
Editors Fiona Duncan and Leonie Glass **Revisions Editor** Hermione Edwards
Art Director Mel Petersen **Designer** Ian Midson
Maps Andrew Green pages 18-27, 52-103, Eugene Fleury pages 14-17, 28-51, 104-127

Photographs Mel and Fiona Petersen

Printed by: Nutech, India

**Visit Duncan Petersen's travel website at
www.charmingsmallhotels.co.uk**

CONTENTS

Exploring Paris on foot

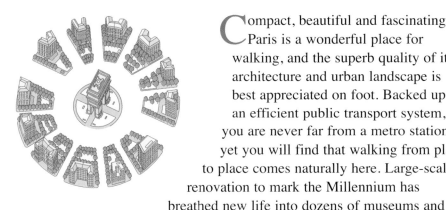

Compact, beautiful and fascinating, Paris is a wonderful place for walking, and the superb quality of its architecture and urban landscape is best appreciated on foot. Backed up by an efficient public transport system, you are never far from a metro station, yet you will find that walking from place to place comes naturally here. Large-scale renovation to mark the Millennium has breathed new life into dozens of museums and historically important buildings. The unveiling of the dazzling Opéra Garnier, to gasps of astonishment, is an indication that many of the city's efforts have been successful. Furthermore, a huge programme of planting has created many new green, flower-filled spaces all over the magical city: there are today no less than 3,075 hectares of public gardens and 6,000,000 trees.

Paris's origins can be found in the very heart of the city – the Ile de la Cité, which a Gallic tribe, the Parisii, made their stronghold on the river. When the Romans supplanted them, the town of Lutetia sprang up, with the governor's palace on the island, and the arena and forum on the Left Bank. Today's city is bounded by a circular road, the Périphérique, and, within, divided into 20 *arrondissements* (districts) which spiral

HOW THE MAPPING WAS MADE

The mapping was originally created from specially-commissioned photographs taken from a helicopter, which flew at about 1,500 feet, with the camera angled at 45°. Weather conditions had to be slightly overcast in order to achieve a maximum level of detail on the buildings.

Scores of enlargements were made from these negatives, which a group of technical illustrators then used to create the maps, working in pen and ink. For this book, the mapping has been developed further: extracted areas have been digitally redrawn and coloured.

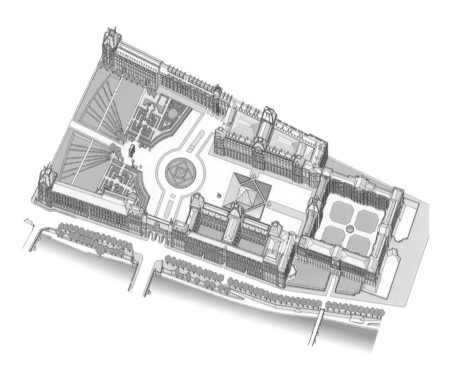

outwards from the centre. Each has its own character, as do the *quartiers* (quarters) – Montmartre, St Germain, Montparnasse, the Latin Quarter and so on. Through the middle flows the Seine; to the north is the Right Bank (Rive Droite), to the south, the Left Bank (Rive Gauche).

The aerial-view – isometric – mapping used to illustrate our walks makes this guide the perfect companion as you explore the city. Streets, parks, squares, even individual buildings are brought to life on the page. There is no need for full directions – the route as marked on these maps is very easy to follow, in conjunction with the maps' numerals, linked to information about places of interest in the text.

The walks are designed to show you the city in all its facets and to give you a taste of a Parisian's Paris. This guide covers all the important districts, sights and much more, beginning with an indispensable introduction to the city on pages 16-17. Thereafter each walk explores in depth the area it covers, revealing interesting museums and galleries, historical details, hidden nooks and crannies, and the best shops, restaurants, cafés, markets and picnic spots. A walk could take you all day to complete, or just a morning. If you follow them all, you will get to know Paris very well.

HOW TO USE THIS BOOK

The area covered by the walks stretches from Montmartre in the north to the Jardin du Luxembourg in the south, and from the Arc de Triomphe in the west to the Bastille in the east.

Using the maps

The route of each walk is clearly marked on the map, with the occasional arrow to keep you heading in the right direction. This guide tells you where the walk starts and finishes, and the nearest metro station – never more than a few minutes walk away.

Numerals on the maps correspond to the numerals in the text, highlighting places of interest and importance. Where only a specific building, the numeral will appear on that building, but where there are several places of interest in the same street, the numeral will normally be placed on that street. The name of the place of main interest appears in bold print. Bold print is also used to highlight other significant places nearby – buildings, museums, galleries, statues, sculptures, restaurants, cafés or shops. Where relevant, opening times are listed, so you can plan a visit to one (or several) of the sights on your walk (for more information on admissions to sights, see page 14).

Montmartre 18-27
Champs-Elysées to Parc de Monceau 72-79
Around the Grands Boulevards 80-87
The Louvre to the Arc de Triomphe 60-71
Bourse to the Opéra 88-95
Palais Royal to Beaubourg 96-103
Musée d'Orsay 36-43
The Marais 104-111
Ile St-Louis and Ile de la Cité 120-127
Bastille 112-119
Les Invalides 52-59
Latin Quarter 28-35
St-Germain and Luxembourg 44-51

LINKING THE WALKS

All the walks are within easy reach of each other (if not by foot, by bus or metro), but there are a number that link specifically. **Shamelessly Chic** finishes at St Sulpice, a short walk away from Odéon and the start of **Left Bank Impressions. Island Hopping** links with **Scholars and Rebels** at place St Michel. After walking **Storming the Galleries,** continue along rue St Antoine to St Paul and the start of **Nobility Regained,** the walk that explores the Marais. Alternatively, head from place de la Bastille down boulevard Henri IV to the start of **Island Hopping.** A walk down avenue de l'Opéra – or two stops on the metro – will link the **Commerce and Culture** walk to **From the Sublime to the Surreal.**

THE WEATHER

August, the month when Parisians traditionally evacuate the city, can be surprisingly and unpleasantly hot, with temperatures soaring as high as 30°C (86°F). The autumn weather is generally mild and warm, and spring often brings clear blue skies, but temperatures can be cool. The winter months are sometimes uncomfortably cold and damp. For weather forecasts in Paris and the Ile de France region, visit the website: www.meteo.france.com

WHEN TO USE THIS BOOK

Most of the walks can be enjoyed at any time of the year, but some – especially those just out of the centre, or those which include parks or gardens or areas where there is a vibrant street life – are more fun to walk when the weather is fine.

SUMMER WALKS

ART AND A PARK: in the heat of the summer, head away from the Champs-Elysées to a picnic in the cool shade of the Parc de Monceau.

ISLAND HOPPING: although they are busier in high season, pick a fine day to explore the islands. Lunch outside a café and climb Notre-Dame. If you wish, tag an hour's river cruise from Pont Neuf onto the end of the walk.

PUTTING ON THE RITZ: the beautiful and unexpected garden in square Louis XVI makes the perfect spot for a picnic lunch on a summer's day.

SECRET GARDENS AND GREAT MANSIONS: this route takes in not just one, but several charming gardens, including the Musée Rodin's, dotted with stunning sculptures.

SHAMELESSLY CHIC: summer is the season for relaxing at a St Germain outdoor café and enjoying the peaceful Luxembourg Gardens to the full.

STORMING THE GALLERIES: in fine weather Village St Paul feels like an open-air market, with all the galleries displaying their wares outside. There is also more river traffic to watch in summer, along the lively and colourful Port de la Plaisance marina.

WINTER WALKS

ARTS AND TARTS: try to visit Montmartre on a sunny winter's day; clear weather is essential to see the view at its best, and in winter you have more chance of avoiding the worst of the crowds.

COMMERCE AND CULTURE: on this walk you can take refuge from the cold and the rain in a network of interlinking *passages*, specifically designed so that people could shop in comfort.

GRAND PARADE: on a chilly day, you can while away time in the Louvre and cheat by doing the route by bus or metro.

LEFT BANK IMPRESSIONS: warm yourself with a hot chocolate at one of boulevard St Germain's famous cafés, and finish with a ramble round the Musée d'Orsay.

NOBILITY REGAINED: on this walk, a host of museums provide shelter from the elements.

WEEKEND WALKS

ART AND A PARK: this route is quieter, its park more fun and its museums are all open at the weekend.

ISLAND HOPPING: a perfect walk for a Sunday, when the *quais* are closed to traffic from 9am to 5pm (from late March to November) and the *bouquinistes* do a roaring trade.

SECRET GARDENS AND GREAT MANSIONS: time this walk – if you can – around the farmers' market in boulevard Raspail, which is only open on Sunday morning. It's fun and you can pick up a picnic here to eat later.

STORMING THE GALLERIES: avoid Tuesday and Wednesday, when the shops, studios and galleries in Village St Paul are closed; come here on a Sunday when they are at their liveliest.

WEEKDAY WALKS

Arts and Tarts: Montmartre is slightly less crowded during the week, but if you want to visit the museum, avoid Monday, when it is closed.

Commerce and Culture: the Bourse is only open for tours between Monday and Friday, and the surrounding area, which buzzes during the week, can be almost deserted at weekends.

Nobility Regained: the Marais attracts visitors in droves on Saturday and Sunday, so do this walk during the week, but not on Monday or Tuesday, when most of the museums are closed.

Putting on the Ritz: the best days for this walk are Thursday, Friday or Saturday, when the Chapelle Expiatoire is open in the afternoon. Avoid Sunday, when most of the shops are closed and shuttered.

Scholars and Rebels: buzzing with chattering students, the Latin Quarter only really shows its true colours during the week in term time.

Shamelessly Chic: it is pointless to attempt this walk for hardened shoppers on a Sunday.

WALKS FOR KIDS

The following walks could be especially enjoyable for children:

Arts and Tarts: where they can't fail to enjoy the Musée en Herbe's innovative exhibitions and workshops designed for children. Small children who can't cope with the climb might relish the funicular ride, and the Montmartrobus (Route 18), which takes visitors all around Montmartre, and stops at the Abbesses metro station.

Commerce and Culture: the maze of passages on this walk is sure to appeal, and the route can be extended to include a visit to the waxworks museum, Musée Grévin.

Grand Parade: don't linger in the Louvre, but concentrate on the Jardin des Tuileries, a ride on the Ferris wheel (if it's still there), a visit to the Palais de la Découverte museum packed with hands-on exhibits, and a climb up the Arc de Triomphe.

Island Hopping: attractions on this walk might include a climb up Notre-Dame to inspect the gargoyles, ice cream from Berthillon, the flower- (or on Sunday, bird-) market and a boat trip from Pont Neuf at the end.

Nobility Regained: young people love the fun, bustling Marais district; there are so many museums and specialist shops, they are bound to find something to interest them.

Scholars and Rebels: kids will lap up the buzzing rue de la Harpe, be entranced by the *Lady with the Unicorn* tapestries in the Musée National du Moyen Age, and be enthralled by the eerie Panthéon with its rooftop panorama. Finish by extending the walk into the atmospheric Jardin des Plantes with its Natural History Museum and its enigmatic zoo.

Shamelessly Chic: with children in tow, skip the shops and make a beeline for the child-friendly Luxembourg Gardens.

From the Sublime to the Surreal: there is a small playground and sandpit at the Palais Royal, while older children will enjoy the spectacular panorama from the top of the Samaritaine department store and the ever-youthful Les Halles and Beaubourg area.

GETTING TO PARIS
Eurostar offers an excellent service from central London to the heart of Paris. For further information or to book, visit www.eurostar.com or call 08705 186 186.

GETTING AROUND
The RATP (Paris's transport authority) operates an efficient and fully-integrated network of underground/subway trains, buses and express trains running out into the suburbs. Look out for the route-finder machines, providing information on the quickest way to reach your destination, by whatever combination of transport suits you. Punch in the relevant data and out will come full details on how to proceed.

The Metro
Paris's underground (or subway) system is rightly admired, and it's the best way of getting about. Service is fast and frequent (trains run at 90 second intervals for much of the day); trains are generally clean and comfortable; and security, once a major problem, is now much improved, with police patrols common at major interchanges. A trip on the metro is often enlivened by buskers, including classical musicians and South American bands. Smoking is banned throughout the network.

Using the Metro
Stations are identified at street level by a large circled "M". Tickets are sold in the entrance halls, either from coin-operated machines or the ticket office. Tickets must then be inserted into a barrier to allow you onto the platform. Train service starts at about 5.15am (a little later on Sundays) and ends at about 1.15am. Lines are officially numbered but are commonly known by the names of the station at either end of the route and by a colour. These termini are also used on the orange signs indicating a connection to another line (*correspondence*). The system is easily mastered and clear maps in various formats are available at all Metro stations and tourists offices. As stations are spaced close together, and few are far underground, you will find the Metro a convenient way of getting about, even for short hops.

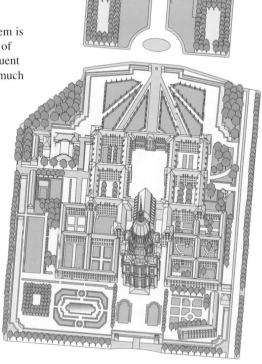

Metro fares

One metro ticket entitles you to travel anywhere in Zones 1 and 2 on the metro and RER trains; tickets can also be used on buses. For RER (fast commuter trains) trips outside the centre, you need special tickets. A variety of bus and metro tickets are sold: your best bet is to buy a *carnet* of ten; a single ticket costs roughly half that of a *carnet* ticket. Only purchase one of the daily, weekly or monthly passes on offer if you are sure you will use the metro frequently. The Week Carte provides two trips per day for six days.

Buses

The existence of bus lanes on many roads in central Paris means that buses move reasonably fast, except during the evening rush hour (about 6 to 8pm). They are a good way of seeing the city, with some positively scenic routes, such as Nos 24, 29, 69 and 96. Montmartre has its own service, the Montmartrobus.

All buses operate a daytime service from 7am to about 8.30pm Mon-Sat, but only about 20 lines run on Sundays. Some of these also operate an evening service until about 12.30am. And ten Noctambus lines, appropriately indicated by an owl sign, radiate out from the place du Châtelet between 1.30 and 5.30am every night. Clear route plans are posted at bus stops. Full bus maps, with lists of evening and Sunday services, are available from metro stations and tourist offices.

Bus tickets

Metro tickets may be used on buses; journeys by bus are often more expensive than by metro, as each journey requires one, two or occasionally as many as four tickets. Bus-only tickets can be purchased on board. All tickets must be validated by inserting them into the machine by the door on the bus.

Taxis

Paris taxis are ordinary sedans, whose drivers' knowledge of the city ranges from the excellent to virtually non-existent. In theory, they can be hailed in the street when their light is on. In practice, few drivers like stopping for a fare and you will save time by making for a taxi stand. Taxis waiting at the stands at rail stations add a special charge on top of the ordinary metred fare.

Metre rates are more expensive between 7.30pm an 7am, at all times on Sundays and public holidays, and when you travel outside the city limits. It is standard practice to add a tip of 10-15 percent on top of the fare. Few drivers will take a passenger in the front seat, which limits you to three adults per cab; if a fourth person is allowed in, an extra charge will be made. Taxis can be ordered by telephone: try Taxis Bleus, tel. 08 91 70 10 10 or Alpha, tel. 01 45 85 85 85.

Unlicensed taxis are best avoided, as prices are steep and drivers may not be fully insured. If you are desperate and cannot afford to wait in the queue for licensed taxis, always agree on a price before getting in to a private cab.

TIPPING

Bars, restaurants and hotels all include 15 percent for service and taxes in their prices (*service compris*), so tipping is not widely practiced in France today. If, however, the service has been particularly good, you can show your appreciation by leaving a small extra amount for the waiter. Small tips should be given to cloakroom attendants and doormen. Airport and railway porters have a fixed charge per item, and taxi drivers will expect 12-15 percent.

TOURIST INFORMATION

The city's main tourist office is at:

• 27, rue des Pyramides, 75001; tel. 08 92 68 30 00 (open Mon-Sat 10am-7pm, Sun and holidays 11am-7pm).

There are additional tourist information bureaux at:

• Eiffel Tower (open Mar-Oct daily 11am-6.40pm).

• Espace du Tourisme en Ile de France, Carrousel du Louvre, 99 rue de Rivoli, 75001 (open daily 10am-6pm).

• Gare de Lyon, by the main exit (open Mon-Sat 8am-6pm).

• Gare du Nord, international arrivals concourse (open daily 8am-6pm).

• Montmartre, 21 Place du Tertre, 75018 (open daily 10am-7pm)

For more information, visit the websites www.parisinfo.com and www.paris-ile-de-france.com.

USEFUL TELEPHONE NUMBERS

Children

For information on events and attractions for children, visit the Centre d'Information et de Documentation pour la Jeunesse (101 quai Branly, 75015; tel. 01 44 49 12 00) or contact the Ministère de la Culture (3 rue de Valois, 75001; tel. 01 40 15 80 00).

Disabled visitors

Disabled visitors can receive guidance from the Comité National Français Liaison Réadaptation des Handicapés (236B rue Tolbiac, 75013; tel. 01 53 80 66 66) or from the Association des Paralysés de France (17 boulevard Blanqui, 75013; tel. 01 40 78 69 00). Useful guides include *Access in Paris*, available through RADAR in London (tel. 020 7250 3222), and *Tourisme pour Tout le Monde* from the tourist office. Escort services are provided or all transport by Les Compagnons du Voyage (visit the website www.compagnons.com, tel. 01 53 11 11 12).

Sightseeing tours

Bus tours of the city are organized by the following companies: Les Cars Rouges (tel. 01 53 95 39 53), Cityrama (tel. 01 44 55 60 00), Paris L'Open Tour (tel. 01 42 66 56 56/7) and Paris Vision (tel. 01 42 60 30 01). Most start in the centre, and take about two hours. On some you can get off at the sights and pick up another bus later. Walking tours are organized by the Caisse Nationale des Monuments Historiques (tel. 01 44 61 21 50), Paris Walking Tours (tel. 01 48 09 21 40) and Paris Contact (tel. 01 42 51 08 40). For a bird's eye view of Paris, Hélifrance (tel. 01 45 54 95 11) arranges helicopter trips from the Paris Héliport at 4 avenue de la Porte-de-Sèvres, 75015.

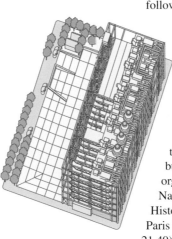

River and canal trips

Two types of boat take visitors on Seine cruises: the huge, glass-encased *bateaux mouches* and smaller, friendlier *vedettes*. The companies that run them are Bateaux-Mouches from Pont de l'Alma (tel. 01 42 25 96 10); Bateaux Parisiens (tel. 01 44 11 33 44) which has a Notre-Dame cruise in summer only from Porte de Montebello and an Eiffel Tower cruise from Pont d'Iena; Vedettes de Paris et de l'Ile de France from Pont d'Iena (tel. 01 47 05 71 29); and Vedettes du Pont Neuf from square du Vert-Galant (tel. 01 46 33 98 38). Batobus (tel. 01 44 11 33 99) runs a water shuttle service between the Eiffel Tower and Notre-Dame, stopping at important sights, such as the Musée d'Orsay and Louvre en route. Canal trips can be arranged through Canauxrama (tel. 01 42 39 15 00) or the Paris Canal Company (tel. 01 42 40 96 97).

Useful publications

To find out what's on in Paris, buy one of the weekly listings magazines *Pariscope* or *L'Officiel des Spectacles*, which come out on Wednesday and are available from news stands. *Pariscope* contains a useful section in English, Time Out Paris. You can pick up a copy of the *Time Out Paris Free Guide*, published quarterly, in most hotels, American Express and tourist offices, and the *Time Out Eating and Drinking Guide*, a comprehensive guide to restaurants, cafés and bars, is available from English bookshops.

Theatre tickets

Buy tickets direct from the theatre box office, in person, by telephone or by post. Alternatively, you can buy them from FNAC stores (Forum des Halles, 1 rue Pierre-Lescot, 75001; 26 avenue des Ternes, 75017; and branches throughout Paris), and Virgin Megastore (52-60 avenue des Champs-Elysées, 75008). Half-price tickets are sold on the day of performance at

---

Kiosque Théâtre at 15 Place de Madeleine (open Tues-Sun 12.30-8pm) and Montparnasse station (open Tues-Sun 12.30-8pm).

Opening times

The walks in this book pass many museums and monuments. Consider purchasing a *Paris Carte-Musée* (from museums and main metro stations), which gives unlimited access and allows you to bypass wearysome queues.

Most museums close on a Monday or Tuesday. Some of the smaller ones close over lunch, and some in August. Museums and monuments with extended opening hours include the Louvre, open until 9.45pm on Wednesday and Friday, and the Eiffel Tower, open until 10.30pm (11pm July and August). Some museums are half-price or free on Sundays.

So that you can plan when best to do each walk, we mention the day(s) of the week that each museum is closed, and opening hours if they are unusual.

Luggage storage and lost property

The central office for lost property is at 36 Rue des Morillons, 75015 (open Mon, Wed and Fri 8.30am-5pm, Tues and Thur 8am-8pm.) There are luggage storage facilities at all major rail stations.

Shopping and banking hours

Generally speaking, shops in central Paris open at 9 or 10am and close at 7pm. Specialty food stores and other small shops often close for lunch from about noon to 3 or 4pm, and many local stores close on Monday. Most department stores are open till 10pm on Thursdays. Most restaurants close one day a week, many on Sunday, and many in August. Fashion shops may also shut down during high summer.

Banking hours are roughly from 9am to 4.30pm, but exchange counters may close between noon and 2pm. All banks close at lunchtime the day before a public holiday.

WALKING SAFELY

Crossing busy roads can be hazardous even on zebra crossings, where drivers are supposed to give way but often don't. The motto in Paris is walk with confidence, so follow the Parisians' example. The only people dithering on the boulevards are foreign visitors. A few outer areas are unsafe for pedestrians after nightfall: if outside the city centre after dark, make sure you stick to the well-lit main streets.

There are numerous bureaux de change throughout the city, which are usually open on Sundays. Also open daily are bank branches at the Austerlitz, Est, Nord and St Lazare rail stations. The UBP at 154 avenue des Champs-Elysées is open at weekends. Cash dispensers (ATMs) are found all over the city.

Private bureaux de change, usually offering less favourable rates, are particularly common in the St Germain-des-Prés district.

Public holidays

Many museums and tourist sights, and most shops, are closed on: New Year's Day, Easter Monday, 1 May (Labour Day), 8 May (VE Day), Feast of Ascension (6th Thurs after Easter), Whit Monday (2nd Mon after Ascension), 14 July (national holiday to commemorate the storming of the Bastille), 15 August (Feast of the Assumption of the Virgin Mary), 1 November (All Saints Day), 11 November (Remembrance Day) and Christmas Day.

Introducing Paris on Foot

This walk is designed as an introduction to the city, to help you to find your bearings and give you a first glimpse of the most important sights, many of which you can return to in other walks. It will take you about half a day, depending on whether you decide to visit any of the sights along the way. The route follows a wide spiral around the heart of the city, taking you from the Right Bank to the Left and then back again. Leading you down narrow side streets and along broad boulevards, this walk includes a host of well-known landmarks. This is the walk to do if you are in Paris for a quick visit and only have time for one. With a few changes, you can also do the entire route by bus.

Palais Royal, now the Conseil d'Etat.

Start at place de l'Opera, a main intersection at the core of Baron Haussmann's grand design for the city. The square is overshadowed by the exuberant **Opéra Garnier,** glittering since its recent restoration (see **Commerce and Culture,** p.95). Walk southwest down the bustling boulevards des Capucines and de la Madeleine to **place de la Madeleine,** ringed by exotic food shops, where the Neoclassical **La Madeleine** church stands four-square like a great Roman relic (see **Putting on the Ritz,** p.83).

Head straight down **rue Royale,** indulging in some exclusive window-shopping as you go, to **place de la Concorde** (see **Grand Parade,** p.66). As you pass between a pair of magnificent Louis XV buildings, the one on your right is now home to the smart **Hotel Crillon.** Cross the Seine via Pont de la Concorde opposite the Assemblée Nationale (the French parliament), which occupies the Palais-Bourbon, originally built by one of Louis XIV's daughters but now sporting a Greek-style façade added by Napoleon.

Turn left along quai Anatole-France and walk down to the **Musée d'Orsay,** a stylish museum with the world's greatest collection of Impressionist paintings housed in an old railway station (see **Left Bank Impressions,** p.42). Continue along the *quai* and turn right into rue du Bac, packed with antique shops and galleries. Walk on until you reach **boulevard St Germain,** the main artery of the Left Bank and an excellent place to stop for a coffee or for lunch.

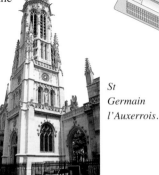

St Germain l'Auxerrois.

Just past the church of St Germain-des-Prés (see **Left Bank Impressions,** p.40), turn left into **rue de Buci,** scene of an open-air fruit and vegetable market in the morning (Tuesday-Friday) and home to a galaxy of art galleries, book and antique shops. Follow rue de Buci, which becomes rue St André-des-Arts, to **place St Michel,** hub of the Latin Quarter (see **Scholars and Rebels,** p.30).

Pont au Double takes you across the river to the **Ile de la Cité** and a glimpse of the magnificent medieval cathedral of **Notre-Dame** (see **Island Hopping,** p.125). Return to the Right Bank by Pont d'Arcole. Head up rue du Renard, passing the ornate 19thC

Renaissance-style **Hôtel de Ville** on your right and the haunting Gothic **Tour St Jacques** on your left. Ahead to the left lies high-tech exhibition space, the **Pompidou Centre** (see **From the Sublime to the Surreal,** p.103), overlooking a colourful piazza. Take the escalator up to the top for a terrific view.

Walk west along rue Berger, past the exquisite 16thC **Fontaine des Innocents** on your left, to The **Forum des Halles** (see **From the Sublime to the Surreal,** p.102), built here on the site of a bustling food market, with origins dating back to the 12th century. Turn left down rue du Pont Neuf and then right into elegant, colonnaded rue de Rivoli, lined with luxurious shops. Walk towards the Louvre (see **Grand Parade,** p.64), and even if you don't have time to go inside, walk down to the main (west) entrance for a sight of I.M. Pei's glass and steel pyramid. Leave via the attractive Louvre-Rivoli metro station, decorated with bas-reliefs and statues.

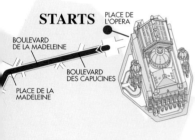

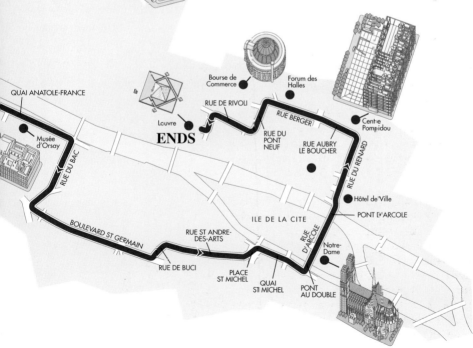

Arts and Tarts: Montmartre

▶ **STARTS**
Place des Abbesses. Nearest metro: Abbesses.

■ **ENDS**
Place des Abbesses. Nearest metro: Abbesses.

Memorial to the singer, Yolanda Gigliotti, known as Dalida.

Even if you take the funicular up Montmartre's hill, the Butte, you can't avoid some climbing, so this is a walk for the fit. The district's name, from *mons martyrium* (mount of martyrs), commemorates the martyrdom of St Denis with two companions in AD250. For centuries it was a rural village, bristling with the windmills that ground the capital's flour. In the 19th century its picturesque charm and low rents were discovered by artists, writers and musicians. Their arrival heralded the opening of lively bars, raucous cabarets and sleazy bordellos, prerequisites of *la vie de bohème*. Montmartre's heyday was in the late 19th and early 20th centuries, when Picasso lived in Le Bateau Lavoir and Utrillo drank absinthe at the Lapin Agile, both included in this walk. The tourists arrived with World War I, and today make their pilgrimage up the Butte in droves, congregating in the original village square, place du Tertre, and around Sacré-Coeur, still a powerful icon despite years of exploitation. There is a notoriously seedy side to Montmartre, particularly around Pigalle, but in its backwaters – little squares, winding streets, old cemeteries – it has clung on to its village atmosphere and charm.

Carved frieze above a Montmartre doorway.

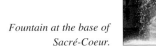

Fountain at the base of Sacré-Coeur.

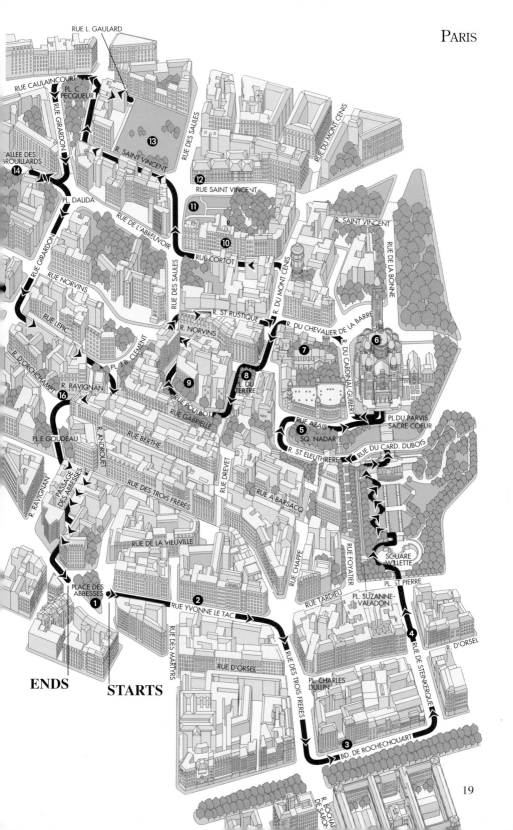

RUE L. GAULARD

RUE CAULAINCOURT

PL. C PECQUEUR

RUE GIRARDON

ALLEE DES BROUILLARDS

14

13

R. SAINT VINCENT

RUE DES SAULES

RUE DU MONT CENIS

PL. DALIDA

12

RUE SAINT VINCENT

R. SAINT VINCENT

RUE DE L'ABREUVOIR

11

RUE GIRARDON

RUE NORVINS

RUE DES SAULES

10

RUE CORTOT

R.

RUE DE LA BONNE

RUE LEPIC

PL. J.B. CLEMENT

R. ST RUSTIQUE

R. NORVINS

R. DU MONT CENIS

R. DU CHEVALIER DE LA BARRE

6

R. D'ORCHAMPT

R. RAVIGNAN

16

9

RUE FOULBOT

PL. DU TERTRE

8

7

R. DU CARDINAL-GUIBERT

PL. GOUDEAU

R. ANDROUET

RUE BERTHE

RUE GABRIELLE

RUE AZAIS

SQ. NADAR

5

R. ST ELEUTHRERE

PL. DU PARVIS SACRE-COEUR

RUE DU CARD. DUBOIS

R. RAVIGNAN

PASSAGE DES ABBESSES

RUE DES TROIS FRERES

RUE DREVET

RUE A BARSACQ

RUE DE LA VIEUVILLE

RUE CHAPPE

RUE FOYATIER

SQUARE WILLETTE

PLACE DES ABBESSES

1

RUE YVONNE LE TAC

2

PL. ST PIERRE

PL. SUZANNE-VALADON

RUE TARDIEU

RUE DES MARTYRS

RUE D'ORSEL

RUE DES TROIS FRERES

PL. CHARLES DULLIN

RUE DE STEINKERQUE

4

R. D'ORSEL

ENDS

STARTS

3

BD. DE ROCHECHOUART

R. BOCHA DE SARON

19

❶ As you come out of the metro into the picturesque **place des Abbesses,** glance back at the seductive curves of the pale green ironwork and glazed roof of its perfectly preserved Belle Epoque entrance. An early design by Hector Guimard, it is one of only two surviving originals. The square is named after the nuns for whom Adelaide of Savoy, wife of Louis VI ('the Fat'), founded a women's abbey at the summit of the Butte in 1133. Tired of the climb to the abbey, the nuns moved down here in the 17th century. On the south side is Anatole de Baudot's Moorish church of **St Jean-l'Evangéliste** (1904), the first in the city to be built of reinforced concrete. Its ceramic decoration and red-brick facing have earned it the affectionate nickname 'St Jean-des-Briques'.

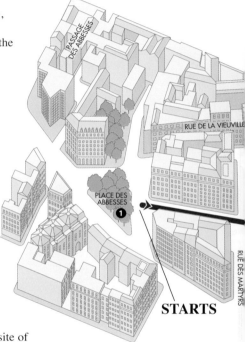

Metro entrance in place des Abbesses.

St Jean-l'Evangéliste church.

❷ Leave the square by **rue Yvonne Le Tac,** lined with restaurants and galleries – some doubling as both. Legend has it that this is the site of the martyrdom of St Denis, brought here by Roman soldiers to be executed at the hilltop Temple of Mercury. Too exhausted to complete the climb, the soldiers decapitated him halfway up the hill, whereupon Denis picked up his severed head and staggered on for another 4 miles (6 km), stopping only to wash it under a nearby fountain. He finally collapsed on the spot where the basilica of St Denis now stands. The 19thC **Chapelle du Martyre,** on the site of his execution, replaced an earlier chapel where the Jesuit Order was founded in 1534. (Crypt open Thurs pm.)

A short way down rue des Trois Frères, the road opens out into the shady, cobbled **place Charles Dullin** with the handsome **Théâtre de l'Atelier** at its far end and **Café du Théâtre,** a possible coffee stop.

STARTS

Théâtre de l'Atelier.

3 The walk brings you down to bustling boulevard de Rochechouart, not for its charm – it has little – but for historical interest. No. 84 is now a tacky souvenir shop, but it once housed **Le Chat Noir,** Rodolphe Sasis' cabaret. Here members of the bourgeoisie could make brief but exciting excursions away from their staid lives to rub shoulders with a bohemian *demi-monde*. A few doors away, the superb, if crumbling, Art Nouveau façade of the **Théâtre Elysée-Montmartre** still stands at No. 72. In its heyday, this nightclub was unrivalled for the extravagance of its decoration and shows. It was here that the famous can-can dancer La Goulue made her debut before defecting to the Moulin Rouge.

Théâtre Elysée-Montmartre.

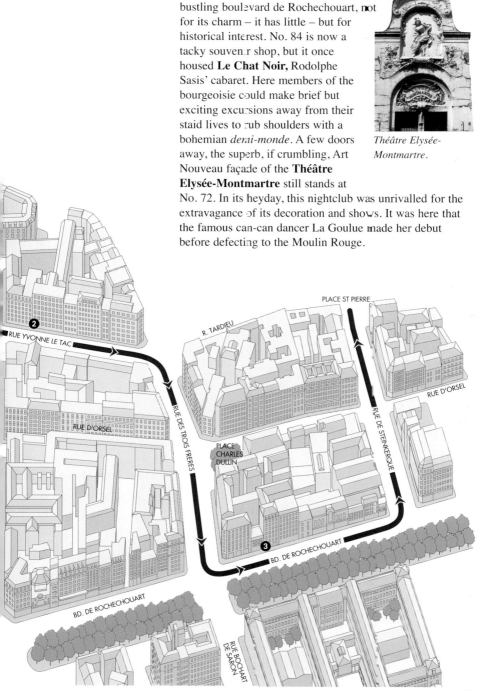

4 Bargain fabric and clothes shops line **rue de Steinkerque,** whose brothels were frequented by the young Pablo Picasso. As you near the top, the familiar wedding-cake outline of the Sacré-Coeur basilica comes into view. To the right of square Willette, Halle St Pierre (off map) is home to the **Musée d'Art Naïf Max Fourny,** a stunning international collection of naïve paintings and sculptures; the **Musée en Herbe,** a children's museum dedicated to conservation; and a useful café. (Open daily.)

Fabric shop display.

The steps up to the basilica thread between immaculate lawns and are bordered by hedges. Well-placed benches invite you to sit, get your breath back and admire the growing view. If you can't manage the climb, take the **funicular** from place Suzanne-Valadon.

Shop sign.

5 Walk past the precipitous rue Foyatier steps (266 altogether) and on to leafy **square Nadar,** presided over by a statue of Chevalier de la Barre, a 19-year-old knight who in 1766 was cruelly punished for singing songs in front of a procession of Capuchin friars without doffing his hat. He was executed, but only after his tongue had been pulled out, his hand cut off and his body burned. The street that curls around the back of the basilica is named after him.

6 When you reach the **Basilique du Sacré-Coeur,** which runs the Eiffel Tower a close second in the popularity stakes, walk to the edge of the **place du Parvis** and just enjoy the view. From this vantage point the stunning city unfolds before you – the Eiffel Tower, Les Invalides, Panthéon, Notre-Dame. If you have difficulty in locating the buildings, check the panoramic map to the right of the steps. Impressive rather than beautiful, the vast Romano-Byzantine basilica was designed by Paul Abadie as a symbol of contrition after France's defeat in the Franco-Prussian War. Its construction took decades; the first stone was laid in 1875 but it was not consecrated until 1919. Inside, your eye is drawn to the immense mosaic of Christ with arms outstretched in welcome. If you have a head for heights, climb the narrow twisting stairs to the **dome** and a breathtaking 360-degree panorama over Paris.

7 Montmartre's other church, **St Pierre,** is one of the oldest in Paris, and a remnant of the 12thC Benedictine Abbey. Although a jumble of styles – four supposedly Roman pillars, 12thC choir, 15thC nave, 18thC tower and 20thC doors, the whole is refreshingly simple. There are 85 graves in its tiny churchyard, the **Cimetière Calvaire,** which is only open to the public on 1 November, All Saints' Day or the Day of the Dead.

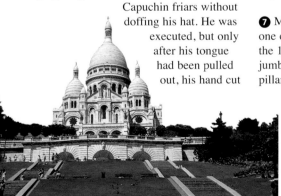

Basilique du Sacré-Coeur.

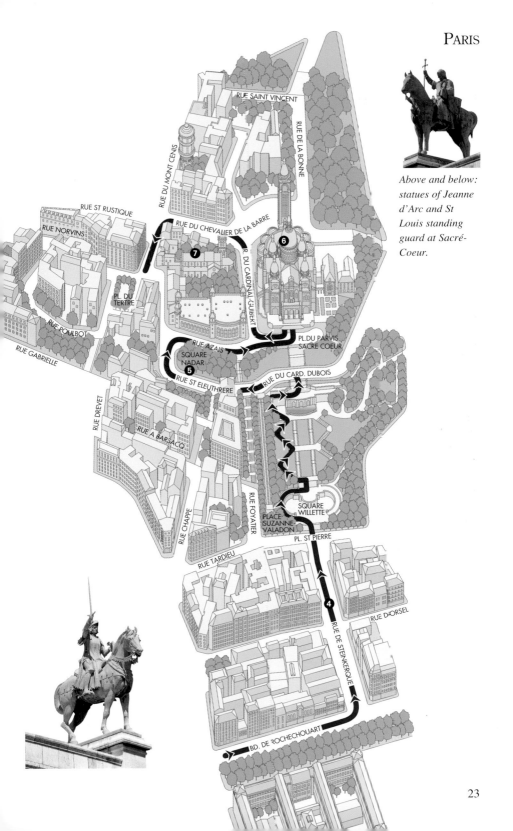

Above and below: statues of Jeanne d'Arc and St Louis standing guard at Sacré-Coeur.

RUE SAINT VINCENT

RUE DE LA BONNE

RUE DU MONT CENIS

RUE ST RUSTIQUE

RUE NORVINS

RUE DU CHEVALIER DE LA BARRE

7

6

R. DU CARDINAL GUIBERT

PL. DU TERTRE

RUE POULBOT

RUE GABRIELLE

RUE AZAIS

PL. DU PARVIS SACRE COEUR

SQUARE NADAR

5

RUE ST ELEUTHRERE

RUE DU CARD. DUBOIS

RUE DREVET

RUE A BARSACQ

RUE CHAPPE

RUE FOYATIER

SQUARE WILLETTE

PLACE SUZANNE VALADON

PL. ST PIERRE

RUE TARDIEU

4

RUE D'ORSEL

RUE DE STEINKERQUE

BD. DE ROCHECHOUART

23

Art for sale in place du Tertre.

8 Even on the chilliest of days, you will have to battle your way through the throngs of tourists in the 14thC **place du Tertre.** Here in the famous square at the heart of Montmartre, travelers come willingly to be ripped off by undistinguished artists, whose vulgar landscapes and portraits are displayed in every available niche. It was in the 19th century that the square became popular as an exhibition space, but standards have dropped with passing decades. Cuisine is secondary to atmosphere in the brasseries that line the square. Of these, **Chez La Mère Catherine** (No. 6; tel. 01 46 06 32 69), which opened in 1793 and bears the name of its first *patronne*, is the oldest. Leave the square via rue du Calvaire, and walk past another steep set of steps, turning right into **rue Poulbot.**

Cottage in rue Poulbot.

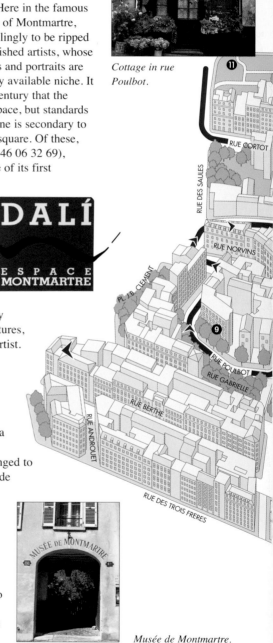

9 Bronze clocks melt over slender branches and a unicorn draws blood from a heart-shaped hole in a wall at **Espace Montmartre Salvador Dali** (No. 11), a cavernous subterranean gallery featuring a permanent exhibition of sculptures, paintings and drawings by the surrealist artist. (Open daily, 10am-6pm.)

10 The district's oldest house, **Musée de Montmartre** takes visitors on an imaginative ramble through its history, including some riveting photographs and a reconstruction of the bohemian Café de l'Abreuvoir. In the 17th century this belonged to Claude de la Rose, better known as Rose de Rosimond, one of Molière's actors. In a strange twist of fate, the actor died (like his boss) on stage while performing *Le Malade Imaginaire*. In the 19th century artists rented studios in the house, among them Renoir, Dufy, Suzanne Valadon (an acrobat and model-turned-expressionist-painter) and her son, Maurice Utrillo, who immortalized **La Maison Rose,** the little pink house at 2 rue de l'Abreuvoir, in one of his paintings. (Tel. 01 42 57 66 75.)

Musée de Montmartre.

⓫ Stand in rue St Vincent and look up to the **Montmartre vineyard,** one of only two such survivors in Paris. Planted in the 1930s at the instigation of the artist Poulbot, it is a reminder of the time when vines covered the Butte. Approximately 700 bottles of Clos Montmartre are produced every year. Though wine buffs rarely rush to buy this robust red with more than a hint of vinegar, a boisterous *fête* is held here in October to celebrate the harvest.

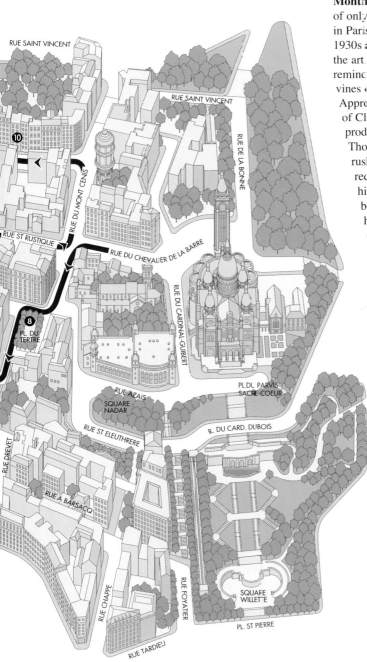

Montmartre vines.

Au Lapin Agile, once favoured by artists and writers.

⑫ Little has changed at the bohemian nightspot, **Au Lapin Agile,** except the clientele. You can still see the pretty terrace shaded by a large acacia, the pink creeper-clad façade, green shutters and André Gill's picture of a rabbit fleeing a saucepan, which – in a roundabout way – gave the place its name (Lapin à Gill). Sadly, tourists have now replaced Allais, Picasso and Utrillo.

⑬ Ivy-covered walls enclose **Cimetière St Vincent** where modest graves lie in the shadow of their flamboyant neighbours. When the Calvaire cemetery was declared full, old Montmartre families who did not have plots in the main cemetery in avenue Rachel, chose this one for their final resting place. Celebrities buried here include Sasis' partner, Emile Goudeau, Marcel Aymé, Gen-Paul and Utrillo. (Open daily.)

⑭ Climb the steps in rue Giradon and make a short detour into **allée des Brouillards** (misty alley), a secret leafy path which lives up to its romantic name. The house on the left is the 18thC **Château des Brouillards,** a rural idyll beloved by artists

and poets. Next, dodge into **square Suzanne Buisson** for a glimpse of the statue of St Denis grimly clutching his severed head.

⑮ Where dozens of windmills once dotted the Montmartre skyline, there are now only two. The handsome clapboard **Moulin du Radet** is less famous than its neighbour **Moulin de la Galette** at No. 79 rue Lepic (off map), which was transformed into a ballroom and featured in the Renoir painting *Le bal du Moulin de la Galette.*

⑯ Originally a piano factory, **Le Bateau Lavoir** became a writers' and artists' colony at the end of the 19th century, when, amongst others, Apollinaire, Picasso, Modigliani and Gris lived and worked in squalid rented rooms. Max Jacob coined its name in 1889, because the building reminded him of one of the laundry boats that plied the Seine. It burned to the ground in 1970, but was reconstructed and now provides more salubrious studio space for aspiring artists. Walk down into the charming **place Emile-Goudeau,** and admire its elegant Wallace fountain (see page 31). You have to be hungry to eat at the rustic 17thC **Relais de la Butte** (12 rue Ravignan; Tel. 01 42 23 24 34), where hearty cheese dishes are standard fare.

Headstone in Cimetière St Vincent.

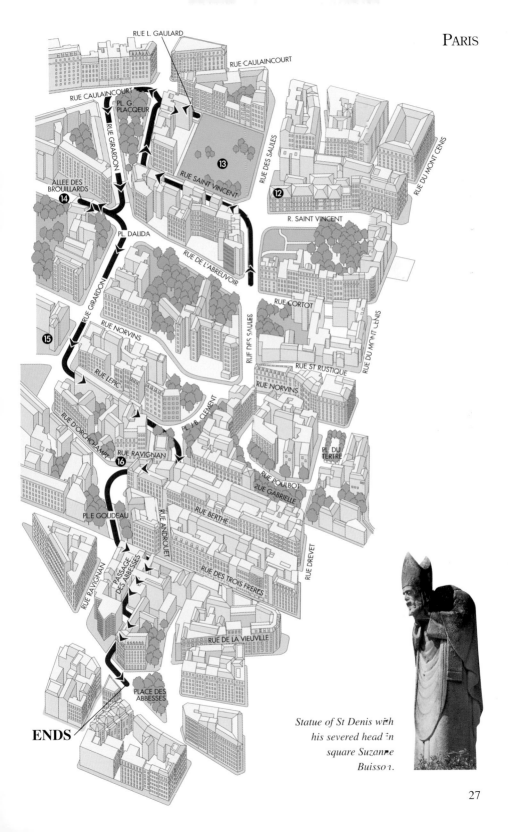

RUE L. GAULARD

RUE CAULAINCOURT

RUE CAULAINCOURT

PL. G PLACQEUR

RUE GIRARDON

RUE DES SAULES

RUE DU MONT CENIS

13

ALLEE DES BROUILLARDS

14

RUE SAINT VINCENT

12

R. SAINT VINCENT

PL. DALIDA

RUE GIRARDON

RUE DE L'ABREUVOIR

RUE CORTOT

RUE DES SAULES

RUE DU MONT CENIS

15

RUE NORVINS

RUE ST RUSTIQUE

RUE DU MONT CENIS

RUE LEPIC

PL. J. B. CLEMENT

RUE NORVINS

RUE D'ORCHAMPT

RUE RAVIGNAN

PL. DU TERTRE

16

RUE POULBOT

RUE GABRIELLE

PLE GOUDEAU

RUE ANDROUET

RUE BERTHE

RUE DREVET

RUE RAVIGNAN

PASSAGE DES ABBESSES

RUE DES TROIS FRERES

RUE DE LA VIEUVLLE

PLACE DES ABBESSES

ENDS

Statue of St Denis with his severed head in square Suzanne Buisson.

27

Scholars and Rebels:
The Latin Quarter

This is the vibrant, rebellious quarter famed both for its scholarship and for its bohemian way of life, where for centuries only Latin was spoken and where political unrest has flared (most notably during the Paris Commune and the student riots of May 1968). It has its roots in the Roman period, and in the Middle Ages became the home of the Sorbonne, the most important centre of learning in France. The district's main artery is boulevard St Michel, known to all as Boul'Mich, but our walk dives away into an enclave of old Roman streets, now a colourful immigrant area. Near the end, we turn from the river to find the fine Musée National du Moyen Age, the Sorbonne, and, finally, the Panthéon high on its hill.

Winged griffin, Fontaine St Michel.

Stories for sale

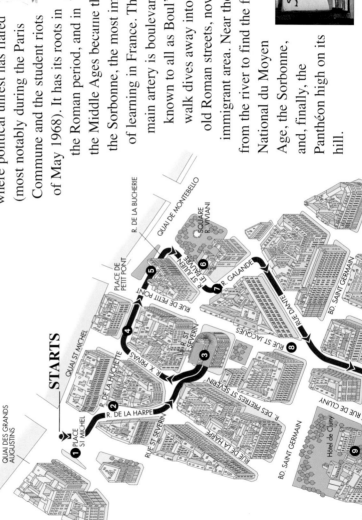

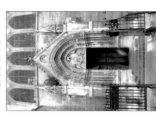

The Gothic church of
St Séverin.

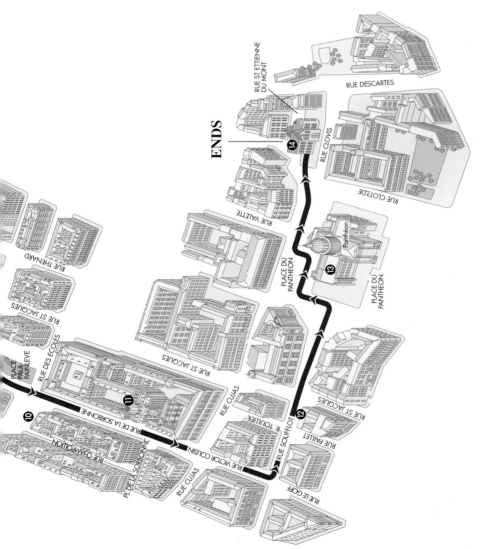

❶ In hectic **place St Michel,** Davioud's Fontaine St Michel (1860) is a magnet for youthful revellers. The entire monument, in which the archangel Michael flings the devil into the waters of the fountain, is slapped up against the lateral wall of the first building in boulevard St Michel.

Fontaine St Michel.

❷ Turn down rue de la Huchette, then branch right along **rue de la Harpe,** plunging, not into a world of learning and Latin, but into a tourist trap of dubious nightspots and cheap Greek and North African restaurants. Smarmy proprietors stand in doorways, entreating every passer-by to enter, ready to pounce at the first sign of weakness. It's like walking the gangplank; don't be tempted to stop unless you are starving.

STARTS

❶ PLACE ST MICHEL

On the door at St Séverin.

❸ For a total contrast, turn left down rue St Séverin and escape into the calm, harmonious Flamboyant Gothic church of **St Séverin.** One's eye is immediately drawn to its finest feature, the double ambulatory, which spills out in a forest of columns from its twisted centre. The church has a peaceful garden, whose curved, pointy-roofed arcade happens to be the only charnel house (burial vault) left in the city, dating from the late 15th century.

❹ Retrace your steps, then turn up rue Xavier-Privas to rejoin **rue de la Huchette.** Notice as you pass grungy **rue du Chat-Qui-Pêche,** distinguished for being the narrowest street in Paris and a reminder of what the medieval city must have felt like; and **No. 10,** where, in 1795, a young, impecunious Napoleon rented a room. Searching in vain for a plaque to confirm the fact, we were reassured by the owner of the nearest *ersatz* taverna (anxious for our business), that Napoleon had indeed lived there, and eaten in his restaurant to boot. Just beyond is the once-hot jazz cellar, **Caveau de la Huchette.**

Caveau de la Huchette.

QUAI DES GRANDS AUGUSTINS

RUE DE LA HARPE

BD. SAINT GERMAIN

Walt Whitman at Shakespeare and Company.

5 Emerging from the tacky enclave, a fine sight appears: Notre-Dame (see page 125) in all its scrubbed and pristine glory. At No. 37 rue de la Bûcherie is the bohemian, atmospheric English-language bookshop **Shakespeare and Company** (midday-midnight daily), until recently run by American George Whitman. It was first started by Silvia Beach as a meeting place of expatriate literati such as Hemingway, Joyce, Pound and Miller. Outside is a **Wallace Fountain,** one of many fountains donated to Paris by Sir Richard Wallace in 1872.

Wallace Fountain in rue de la Bûcherie.

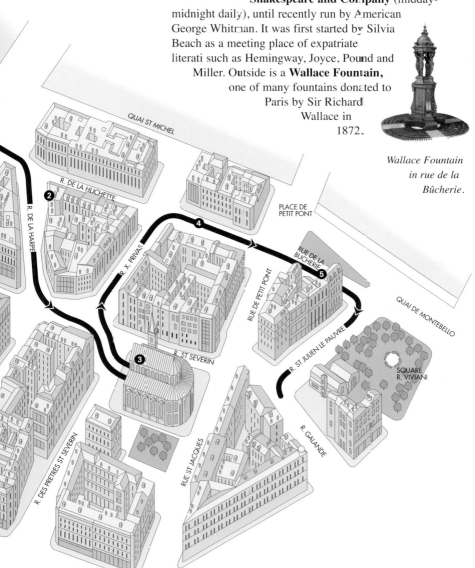

31

6 Set in a pretty garden, with superb views of Notre-Dame, the little church of **St Julien-le-Pauvre** has great appeal and a charmingly rural feel. Modest, unaffected and very old (it was begun in 1170) it seems miles from the centre of Paris. Its simple interior has elegantly foliated capitals on the pillars and, now being a Greek Orthodox church (Melchite sect), Byzantine flourishes. Rue St Julien-le-Pauvre has several old houses with exposed timber beams: notice the fine 17thC portal at No. 14.

Portal, No. 14 rue St Julien-le-Pauvre.

7 Turn left into **rue Galande,** where, on an incongruously scruffy cinema wall, you find the city's oldest street sign, a 14thC bas-relief of St Julien and his wife helping Christ across the Seine. Turn right into rue Dante where **Librairie Gourmande** – a treasure trove of books about food and wine – is busy with Parisians demanding all sorts of culinary tips. Next door is a shop selling cartoon paraphernalia – perfect for Tintin fans.

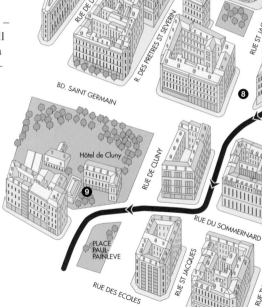

The oldest street sign in Paris, rue Galande.

Sundial by Salvador Dali in rue St Jacques.

❽ In rue St Jacques, look right to see a **sundial by Salvador Dali** on the wall of No. 27, now belonging to a sandwich shop. Rue St Jacques is so named because it marked the start of the medieval pilgrim route to Santiago de Compostela in Spain (St Jacques de Compostelle in French).

❾ Now head for the museum of medieval arts and crafts, the **Musée National du Moyen Age** (formerly Musée de Cluny), where the addition of a medieval garden has made it a delightful place in which to while away time. The museum comprises two buildings: the remains of the Gallo-Roman baths, the **Thèrmes de Lutèce;** and the **Hôtel de Cluny,** a mansion built for the Abbots of Cluny in 1330, rebuilt in 1510. There is much to see: Room 6 is a black square studded with luminous stained glass from Rouen, Ste Chapelle and St Denis. Pierre de Montreuil's stone carved portal of the mid-13th century frames the entrance to a room displaying grave sculpted heads from Notre-Dame.

The unicorn, La Dame à la Licorne.

One is cast back to Roman times in the Frigidarium, a vast room of thermal baths with a 15m high vaulted ceiling. The museum's greatest treasure, however, is the set of six late-15th century tapestries that make up *La Dame à la Licorne.* They conjure up a dreamlike, graceful world inhabited by a mysterious woman, a unicorn, a friendly lion, lady's maids and naughty monkeys. They are at once lyrical, symbolic, romantic, sacred and profane. Five of the tapestries illustrate the five senses and the sixth illustrates (it is thought) the mastery of them. They were discovered in the 19thC by Prosper Mérimée in a château in Creuse, and brought to public attention by the writer Georges Sand. (Closed Tues.)

⑩ Brasserie Balzar (tel. 01 43 54 13 67), a well-known literary haunt, remains one of the most congenial restaurants in Paris, with simple but excellent food, friendly waiters in long white aprons, an interesting mix of diners, wood-panelled walls, vinyl banquettes and plain, old-fashioned charm.

Eglise de la Sorbonne from the Cour d'Honneur.

⑪ At La Sorbonne, founded in the 13th century and now part of the University of Paris, you are in the heart of *Quartier Latin.* Mingle with the students and enter the great courtyard, one side of which is flanked by the Eglise de la Sorbonne, where Cardinal Richelieu (the Sorbonne's 17thC chancellor), is buried. The front of the church faces **place de la Sorbonne,** site of the student riots of May 1968, which fanned out from here.

Victor Hugo in the Sorbonne's Cour d'Honneur.

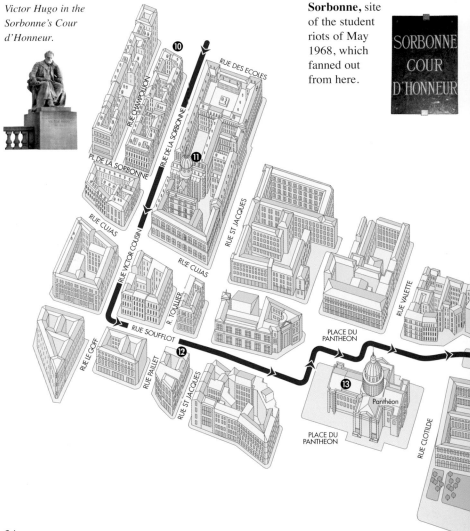

⓬ Compared with the Panthéon hovering above, **Les Fontaines** (tel. 01 43 26 42 80) may look ordinary, but it surprises with its above-average bistro fare – perhaps *carré d'agneau aux herbes de Provence* or *rognons de veau au moutarde de Dijon* – its smiling *patronne* and its bustling atmosphere.

⓭ The hill on which the **Panthéon** sits, Montaigne Ste-Geneviève, was the focal point of the Roman colony of Lutetia, and later named for the patron saint of Paris. The neo-classical church was built by Louis XV as a shrine to Ste Geneviève, but soon changed roles to that of mausoleum for the great dead of France. Chillingly glacial and ghostly inside, with vast expanses of empty floor, it is well suited to its purpose. Around the walls are suitably gruesome scenes, including Joan of Arc burning at the stake and, left of the entrance, St Denis picking up his head to the open-mouthed astonishment of his executioner. The pale, limpid paintings of Puvis de Chavannes are particularly in keeping with the ghostly atmosphere. In the middle, suspended from the dome, is Foucault's Pendulum, recreating the experiment he made in 1851 to prove the rotation of the earth.

Always rather reviled, the Panthéon in fact makes an absorbing place to visit, especially now that you can climb up to the dome for a vertiginous view down into the church, and, from the external colonnade, a breathtaking panorama of Paris. The eerie crypt is full of tombs housed in dark little rooms like prison cells; here are Voltaire, Rousseau, Resistance leader Jean Moulin, Marie and Pierre Curie, Victor Hugo and Emile Zola, who, strange as it may seem, have ended up sharing the same area. (Open daily.)

⓮ The rule-breaking façade of charming **St Etienne-du-Mont** looks as if a child has piled a collection of different shapes one on top of the other to see what effect it makes. Inside is the only remaining rood screen in Paris, dating from 1541, and a richly carved wooden pulpit. Opposite in rue Clovis, the **Lycée Henri IV** stands on the site of the Abbaye Ste Geneviève, founded by King Clovis in the 5th century. Jean-Paul Sartre was on the teaching staff at this well-known secondary school, which fills the Latin Quarter with yet more happy students.

Relief sculpture above the door at St Etienne-du-Mont.

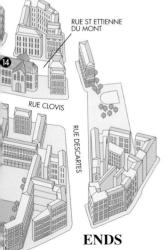

RUE ST ETIENNE DU MONT

RUE CLOVIS

RUE DESCARTES

ENDS

Statue, St Etienne-du-Mont.

Left Bank Impressions: St Germain-des-Prés to Musée d'Orsay

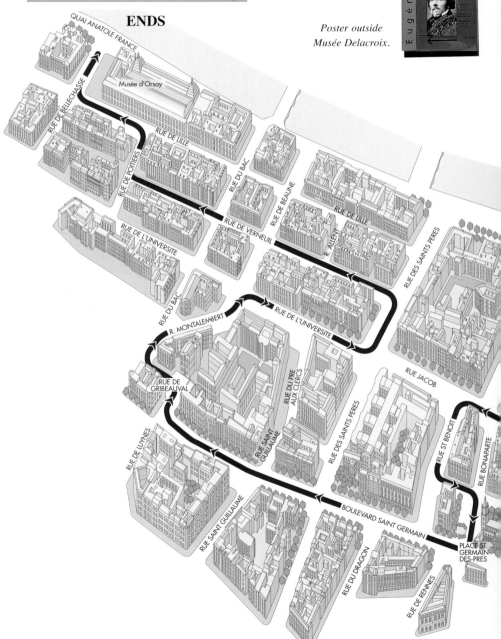

ENDS

Poster outside Musée Delacroix.

Eugène Delacroix

QUAI ANATOLE FRANCE

Musée d'Orsay

RUE DE BELLECHASSE

RUE DE POITIERS

RUE DE LILLE

RUE DU BAC

RUE DE BEAUNE

RUE DE LILLE

RUE DES SAINTS PERES

RUE DE L'UNIVERSITE

RUE DE VERNEUIL

R. ALLENT

RUE DU BAC

R. MONTALEMBERT

RUE DE L'UNIVERSITE

RUE DE GRIBEAUVAL

RUE DU PRE AUX CLERCS

RUE JACOB

RUE DE LUYNES

RUE SAINT GUILLAUME

RUE DES SAINTS PERES

RUE ST BENOIT

RUE BONAPARTE

BOULEVARD SAINT GERMAIN

RUE SAINT GUILLAUME

RUE DU DRAGON

RUE DE RENNES

PLACE ST GERMAIN DES-PRES

▶ **STARTS**
Boulevard St Germain.
Nearest metro: Odéon.

■ **ENDS**
Musée d'Orsay. Nearest
metro: Musée d'Orsay.

Two neighbouring quarters make up the district of St Germain: the ancient St Germain-des-Prés, covering the lands of the medieval monastery and St Germain church, and the more recent (17thC) Faubourg St Germain in the seventh *arrondissement*. This walk

Sandwiches on wheels in rue de Buci.

explores both quarters and the celebrated boulevard that links them. St-Germain-des-Prés has its street market, art galleries and existentialist legacy from the 1950s. Sartre and Simone de Beauvoir's philosophical fireworks at the Café de Flore were a hard act to follow, and although philosophical debates are still held at the Flore, they are organized and lack the sparkle of their predecessors. The smart shopping set moved in with the smart stores, and their Armani carriers have crowded patrons of Shakespeare & Co. out of the cafés. Further north, the Faubourg has some fine houses, but also ambushes you with unexpected moments of visual delight: a glimpse of a leafy courtyard or a flourish of carved stonework. The prize for finishing this walk is the Musée d'Orsay's unmissable French Impressionist collection.

RUE BONAPARTE

R. DES BEAUX ARTS

RUE VISCONTI

RUE. J.CALLOT

RUE DE SEINE

RUE JACOB

R. CARDINALE

RUE DE L'ECHAUDE

RUE DE L'ABBAYE

St Germain-des-Prés

RUE DE BUCI

RUE DE BUCI

RUE GREGOIRE-DE-TOURS

R. DE L'ANCIENNE COMÉDIE

RUE ST ANDRE-DES-ARTS

RUE DU JARDINET

RUE DE L'EPERON

STARTS

COUR DU COMMERCE ST ANDRE

PLACE H. MONDOR

37

❶ Cross boulevard St Germain and turn into cobbled **cour du Commerce St André,** a pocket of history. At the workshop of a German carpenter called Schmidt (No. 9), Dr Louis Guillotin perfected his new inventions in 1792 by experimenting on several unfortunate sheep. Marat's newspaper, *L'Ami du Peuple,* was printed at No. 8; and if you peep through the windows of No. 4, you can glimpse part of a tower from Philip Augustus' medieval city wall. Opposite the back of Le Procope, dive into **cour du Rohan,** three picturesque interlinking courtyards. The middle one preserves its old *pas-de-mule* mounting block and a handsome Renaissance house where Diane de Poitiers, Henri II's mistress, lived.

Statue on roof terrace in rue de Seine.

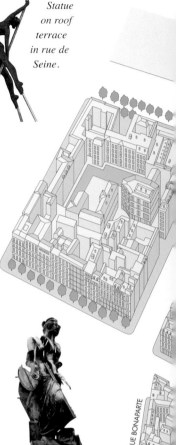

❷ Lively **rue St André-des-Arts** is crammed with bars and bookshops. There's still sawdust on the floor of the old-fashioned bistro, **Allard** (No. 41; tel. 01 43 26 48 23), once frequented by Brigitte Bardot and the Aga Khan and, before that, Racine's residence. Take a short detour down **rue de l'Ancienne Comédie,** where in the 17th century, the Comédie Française performed on an old tennis court at No. 14. **Le Procope** at No. 13 (tel. 01 40 46 79 00), now a chic restaurant, was the first coffee house and a haunt of Molière, Corneille, Voltaire and Balzac. If you retrace your steps and head a short way up rue Mazarine, you'll reach **L'Alcazar** (No. 62; tel. 01 53 10 19 99), outpost of Terence Conran's London restaurant empire: a teeming marble-floored brasserie with a glitzy upstairs bar.

❸ Make sure that you reach **rue de Buci** in the morning, because the street market, where *le tout St Germain* shops for food, packs up at lunchtime (opening again at 4pm). Stalls selling fruit, vegetables, flowers and pastries spill into **rue de Seine.** (Closed Mon, Sun pm.) Head north for the bohemian café **La Palette** at No. 43 (tel. 01 43 26 68 15), its dark-wood walls hung with artists' palettes. An outcrop of art galleries takes over the street as you approach the Ecole des Beaux-Arts.

Statue outside La Palette.

Market stall in rue de Buci.

4 In another street of galleries, **rue des Beaux-Arts,** Oscar Wilde died 'beyond his means' at **L'Hôtel** (No. 13). His bedroom has been preserved almost exactly as it was.

Plaque commemorating Oscar Wilde outside L'Hôtel.

5 Across rue Bonaparte stands the **Ecole Nationale Supérieure des Beaux-Arts,** France's principal school of fine arts, in the impressive 19thC Palais des Etudes, which incorporates part of a 17thC convent built by Marguerite de Valois. Pop in, as there are some fascinating architectural fragments and fine temporary exhibitions to see.

6 Eyecatching from the moment you turn into rue de l'Abbaye, the **Palais Abbatial** was built in 1536 for the St Germain abbot, Charles de Bourbon, who later had a short spell as King Charles X. Avant-garde in its combination of rosy red brick and Paris stone, it was one of the most splendid buildings of its day.

Lamp post outside Palais Abbatial.

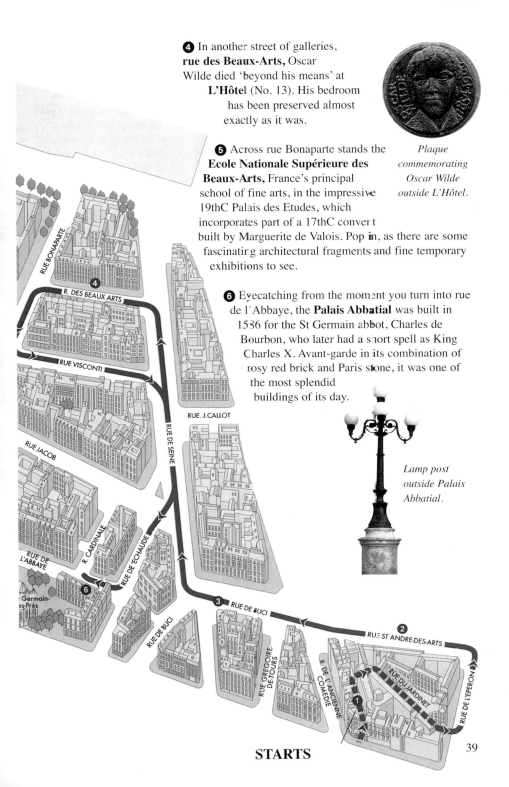

RUE BONAPARTE

4 R. DES BEAUX ARTS

RUE VISCONTI

RUE JACOB

RUE. J.CALLOT

RUE DE SEINE

R. CARDINALE

RUE DE L'ABBAYE

RUE DE L'ECHAUDE

6
Germain-es-Prés

3 RUE DE BUCI

RUE DE BUCI

RUE GREGOIRE-DE-TOURS

R. DE L'ANCIENNE COMEDIE

2 RUE ST ANDRE-DES-ARTS

RUE DU JARDINET

RUE DE L'EPERON

1

STARTS

7 Continue into pretty **place de Fürstemburg,** where the intimate **Musée Delacroix** is devoted to the great 19thC romantic painter who lived, worked and died in this apartment. A charming yet volatile man is revealed through his vivid paintings, letters, photographs and other mementoes. (Closed Tues.) Before you leave this calm corner, glance back to the abbey, a fine sight with its lush garden visible through the wrought-iron gate.

Eugène Delacroix.

8 Return to boulevard St Germain via **rue St Benoît,** a street – like many others in the neighbourhood – whose quiet daytime personality changes after dark, when restaurants turn into jazz clubs and the place starts to buzz (though not quite like its heyday in the Forties and Fifties when Duke Ellington, Charlie Parker and Miles Davis all played the Club St Germain at No. 13). **Petit St Benoît** (No. 4; tel. 01 42 60 27 92) is not one of these. Founded in 1901, it is endearingly old-fashioned with tiled floors, banquettes and robust good-value food.

Tiled panel in rue St Benoît.

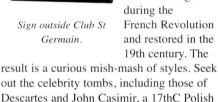

Sign outside Club St Germain.

9 Spend a few moments in the quiet, leafy garden behind the church of **St Germain-des-Prés.** Full of trees, shrubs and birdsong, it harbours a statue by Picasso, *Homage to Apollinaire* – a tribute to his friend, the poet and habitué of the nearby Café de Flore. This church is the oldest in Paris, with origins dating back to AD542, when Childebert I built a basilica here to house holy relics. It stood, surrounded by meadows, at the centre of a colossal estate. After the Normans had destroyed it, the church was rebuilt in the 11th century, only to be vandalized again during the French Revolution and restored in the 19th century. The result is a curious mish-mash of styles. Seek out the celebrity tombs, including those of Descartes and John Casimir, a 17thC Polish king who became abbot of St Germain.

St Germain-des-Prés garden.

Church of St Germain-des-Prés.

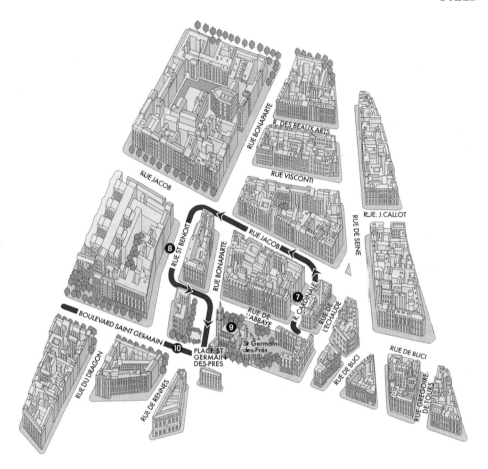

⓾ The district's famous bow-shaped thoroughfare, **boulevard St Germain,** was part of Baron Haussmann's scheme for the city. Though it carved through many of the old Left Bank streets razing a host of fine houses, it soon asserted its own distinctive character. In a colourful stretch, famous rivals **Café de Flore** (No. 172) and **Les Deux Magots** (No. 170) have battled for decades to become the acknowledged home of the intelligentsia. Though once favoured by Hemingway, today the Deux Magots – the name comes from the two Chinese figures perched high on a pillar – seems to be losing out to the shoppers

Statue outside Les Deux Magots.

and tourists. The Flore's wonderful mirrored, red plush and mahogany interior, and the ghosts of Sartre and Simone de Beauvoir still attract the literati – albeit better-heeled than they were when Huysmans, Trotsky and Camus were regulars. Another St Germain institution, Alsatian **Brasserie Lipp** survives at No. 151, its Art Nouveau tiled interior and celebrity clientele intact. But St Germain is undergoing a sea change. Locals still mourn the loss of their seedy 24-hour drugstore at No. 149, replaced by **Emporio Armani** in a triumph of style over bohemia.

⓫ Leave the boulevard, which becomes increasingly residential, for the seclusion of the 17thC **St Thomas d'Aquin** church in its own little square. It was designed in the shape of a Greek cross by Pierre Bullet for the Dominicans whose monastery buildings covered the surrounding streets. Its entrance was on rue St Dominique, where a lovely tree-lined path linked it with the splendid Hôtel de Luynes.

⓬ Across rue du Bac, an extraordinary shop occupies No. 46. **Deyrolle** is a 170-year-old taxidermist, where you can feast your eyes on displays of stuffed animals ranging from a bull to a hummingbird. Children are usually entranced, and eager to spend hours amongst the lambs, goats, Shetland ponies, rats and baby chicks.

⓭ The network of small streets between rue de l'Université and the river at the heart of the old Faubourg St Germain is packed with antique shops and art galleries. These have been dubbed **Le Carré de Rive Gauche,** an organization of 30 dealers, who display its blue and white sign outside their shops. Gorgeous one-off shops specialize in tapestries, carpets, church furniture, china or antiquarian books; more general traders sell anything from a stone sphinx to a silver spoon. Stroll through these streets, window-shopping as you go. Keep a look-out, too, for the secret flower-filled courtyards that lead off the main thoroughfares, like cobbled **cour des Sts Pères** (16 rue des Sts Pères).

⓮ The buzz of conversation will lead you to **Café des Lettres** (No. 53) in part of the 18thC Hôtel d'Avejean, one of the handsome buildings in drowsy **rue de Verneuil.** Owned by the Centre National des Lettres, but open to everyone, this is a perfect spot for a delicious light lunch under an awning in the summer garden.

⓯ Past Antoine Bordelle's two gigantic bronze sculptures in rue de Lille, the **Musée Nationale de la Légion d'Honneur** is dedicated to the history of the tiny red ribbon introduced by Napoleon as France's top award. In Pierre Rousseau's stunning 18thC mansion, the Hôtel de Salm, where Madame de Staël held political salons, you can view splendid displays of medals and insignia, including Napoleon's own medal, sword and breastplate. (Open 2-5 pm, Closed Mon.)

⓰ In Victor Laloux's beautifully restored Gare d'Orsay, a former rail terminus that typified *fin-de-siècle* grandeur, the **Musée d'Orsay** opened in 1986. The art here dates from 1848 to 1914, providing the missing link between the collections in the Louvre (see page 64) and the Pompidou Centre (see page 103). The museum inherited the superb collection of Impressionist paintings from the overcrowded Jeu de Paume, and displays many famous works on its airy, spacious top floor. Exhibits include sculpture, furniture, decorative art, architecture and an exploration of early cinema. Highlights are Rodin's *The Gates of Hell*, Manet's *Le Déjeuner sur l'Herbe*, Van Gogh's *Self-Portrait* and Renoir's exuberant *Moulin de la Galette*. Before leaving the top floor, visit the café behind the vast station clock face, and watch the hands move as you sip your coffee and enjoy the terrific view.

Church of St Thomas d'Aquin.

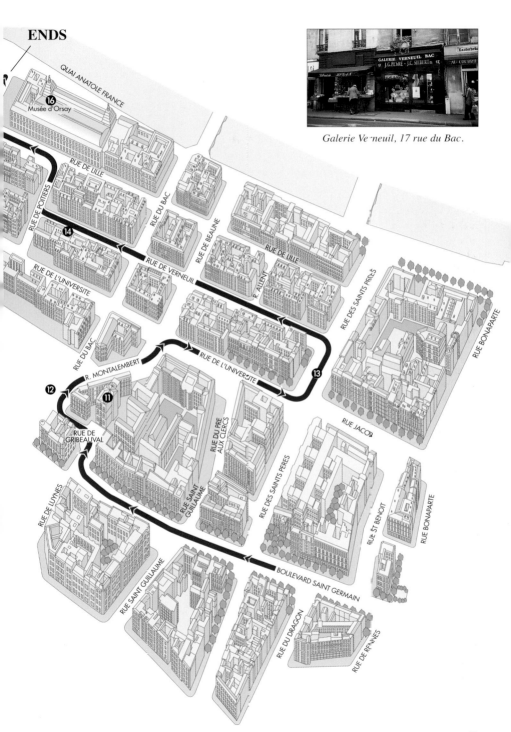

ENDS

QUAI ANATOLE FRANCE

16 Musée d'Orsay

Galerie Verneuil, 17 rue du Bac.

RUE DE LILLE

RUE DE POITIERS

RUE DU BAC

RUE DE BEAUNE

RUE DE LILLE

14

RUE DE VERNEUIL

R. ALLENT

RUE DES SAINTS PÈRES

RUE BONAPARTE

RUE DE L'UNIVERSITE

RUE DU BAC

R. MONTALEMBERT

RUE DE L'UNIVERSITE

13

12

11

RUE DE GRIBEAUVAL

RUE DU PRE AUX CLERCS

RUE JACOB

RUE DE LUYNES

RUE SAINT GUILLAUME

RUE DES SAINTS PÈRES

RUE ST BENOIT

RUE BONAPARTE

RUE SAINT GUILLAUME

BOULEVARD SAINT GERMAIN

RUE DU DRAGON

RUE DE RENNES

Shamelessly Chic: St Germain and Luxembourg

Bathtime luxury.

Although the literati have never moved away from the Left Bank, in recent years the glitterati have joined them, transforming the area between boulevard St Germain and Jardin du Luxembourg into style heaven. The shops, and the people who shop in them, are the epitome of fashionable chic: they ooze style, glamour and understated wealth. The big guns – Dior, Armani, Cartier and the like – have all moved to the Rive Gauche of late, but for shopaholics the area's greatest strength lies in its many imaginative one-off boutiques. Whether you are on a spree or simply window-shopping, it is sheer pleasure to stroll in these pretty streets: gorgeous, impossible clothes are on show at every turn, and there is ample illustration of La Parisienne's obsession with shoes and handbags. The mood of frivolity and sophistication is only enhanced when you reach the Jardin du Luxembourg, a 60-acre oasis (with a café under the trees) which reminds one of a painting by Renoir.

Palais du Luxembourg.

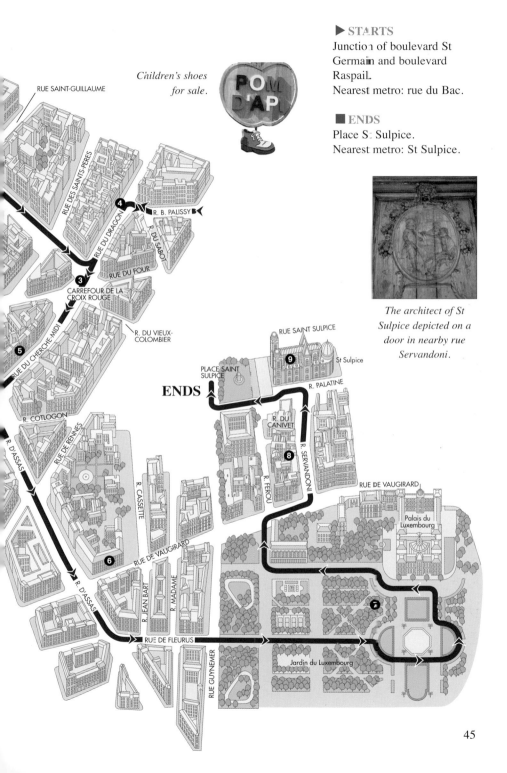

Children's shoes
for sale.

► STARTS
Junction of boulevard St
Germain and boulevard
Raspail.
Nearest metro: rue du Bac.

■ ENDS
Place St Sulpice.
Nearest metro: St Sulpice.

The architect of St
Sulpice depicted on a
door in nearby rue
Servandoni.

RUE SAINT-GUILLAUME

RUE DES SAINTS-PÈRES

RUE DU DRAGON

R. DU SABOT

R. B. PALISSY

RUE DU FOUR

CARREFOUR DE LA
CROIX ROUGE

RUE DU CHERCHE-MIDI

R. DU VIEUX-
COLOMBIER

R. COTLOGON

RUE DE RENNES

R. D'ASSAS

RUE SAINT SULPICE

PLACE SAINT
SULPICE

St Sulpice

ENDS

R. PALATINE

R. DU
CANIVET

R. SERVANDONI

R. FEROU

RUE DE VAUGIRARD

Palais du
Luxembourg

R. CASSETTE

RUE DE VAUGIRARD

R. D'ASSAS

R. JEAN BART

R. MADAME

RUE DE FLEURUS

RUE GUYNEMER

Jardin du Luxembourg

SQUARE DE LUYNES

❶ Take the quiet route to rue de Grenelle by walking along boulevard St Germain (signposted to St Germain-des-Prés), turning right along rue de Luynes, and passing handsome **square de Luynes.** Cross boulevard Raspail and turn right into rue de Grenelle, pausing to inspect one of the best cheese shops in Paris, **Barthélémy.** In a tiny and delicate old shop, ladies in white coats dispense perfect cheeses which M. Barthélémy has personally criss-crossed France to choose. *Le patron* sits in a little cubbyhole in the centre, dispensing advice. Travellers can have their selection wrapped in odour-proof bags (they work: an enormous Brie transported by Eurostar gave off zero smell, despite it being a hot day). Next comes the monumental **Fontaine des Quatres Saisons,** built in 1739 to supply water to the *haute bourgoisie.* Next door is the **Musée Maillol.** Refreshingly cool and tranquil, with stone walls and marble floors, it displays the works

MUSEE MAILLOL

of sculptor Aristide Maillol (1861-1944) donated by his model Dina Vierny, as well as temporary exhibitions. (Open 11am-6pm; closed Tues.)

❷ Retrace your steps and continue along rue de Grenelle. Beyond boulevard Raspail, it dives into the most rarified and chic shopping *quartier* of Paris. Along this particular stretch you will find **Prada, Yohji Yamamoto, Miu Miu** and **Roberto Cavalli.** Or dine at **La Petite Chaise,** the oldest restaurant in Paris (*vraiment!* It dates from 1680; tel. 01 42 22 13 35), with its atmospheric frescoed entrance hall, cramped dining room and friendly *patron*.

Left: outdoor tables, La Petite Chaise.

Bar de la Croix Rouge.

❸ **Carrefour de la Croix Rouge,** the heart of this fashion enclave, is graced by chestnut trees and a well-hung metal *Centaur*, with brushes and tools for a tail. Doubtless laden with purchases in chic carrier bags, you might pause for a coffee in the ever-bustling **Bar de la Croix Rouge.**

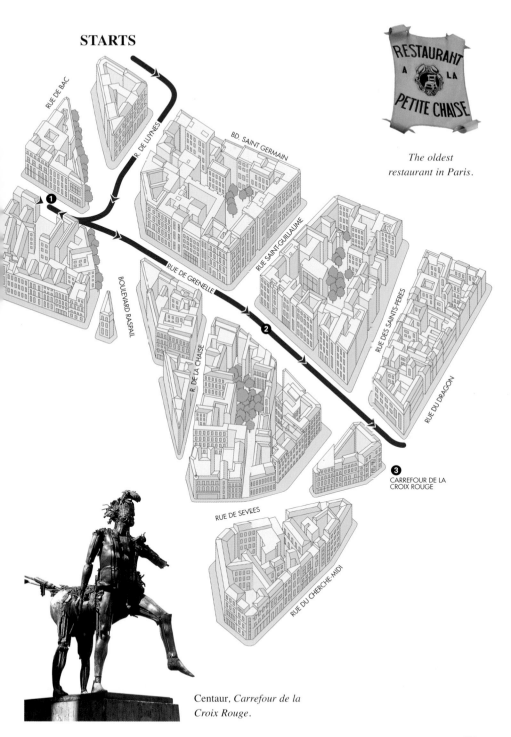

STARTS

RUE DE BAC

R. DE LUYNES

BD. SAINT GERMAIN

RUE SAINT-GUILLAUME

RUE DE GRENELLE

BOULEVARD RASPAIL

R. DE LA CHAISE

RUE DES SAINTS-PÈRES

RUE DU DRAGON

❸ CARREFOUR DE LA
CROIX ROUGE

RUE DE SÈVRES

RUE DU CHERCHE-MIDI

*The oldest
restaurant in Paris.*

RESTAURANT
A LA
PETITE CHAISE

Centaur, *Carrefour de la
Croix Rouge.*

Suitable sign in rue du Dragon.

❹ Stroll along **rue du Dragon,** lined by 17th and 18thC houses, and dip briefly down cobbled **rue Bernard-Palissy** to see a street almost unchanged since those days. Editions de Minuit at **No.7** published Samuel Beckett and nurtured the group of genre-bending 1950s writers whose works became known as the *nouveau roman.*

❺ **Rue du Cherche-Midi** continues the fashion theme, with interesting shops and restaurants all along its narrow length. Join the queues outside **Poilâne,** the city's most famous *boulangerie,* which bakes not the ubiquitous baguette, but the *pain de poilâne*, a great wheel of sourdough bread. If it's Sunday, you will find perfect accompaniments for your bread at the **Marché Biologique** in nearby boulevard Raspail (see page 54).

Stained glass at Poilâne.

❻ In rue d'Assas, glance into the tree-filled courtyard of the **Institut Catholique de Paris,** a presitigious teaching college founded in 1875. Around the corner in Rue Vaugirard the elegant little **St Joseph des Carmes,** part of the Institute's complex, stands on a site once occupied by a great Carmelite monastery with vast gardens and many treasures. During the French Revolution it was turned into a prison where, in 1792, 115 priests and three bishops were massacred. Their shattered remains, disinterred from a mass grave in the garden, are dramatically presented in the crypt. On the opposite corner, **No. 30 rue d'Assas** was the home of Léon Foucault. Here he developed his famous pendulum experiment to demonstrate the rotation of the earth (see page 35). If you want to see the home (from 1903 to 1937) of Gertrude Stein, nip along rue de Fleurus to **No. 27** (ground floor). On the corner, at **Christian Constant,** you might treat yourself to a savoury tart, some salad and a delectable patisserie to eat in the Jardin du Luxembourg (where Gertrude Stein first met Ernest Hemingway).

Courtyard, Institut Catholique de Paris.

GERTRUDE STEIN
1874–1946
ÉCRIVAIN AMÉRICAIN
Vécut ici avec son frère LÉO STEIN puis avec ALICE B. TOKLAS elle y reçut de nombreux artistes et écrivains de 1903 à 1938

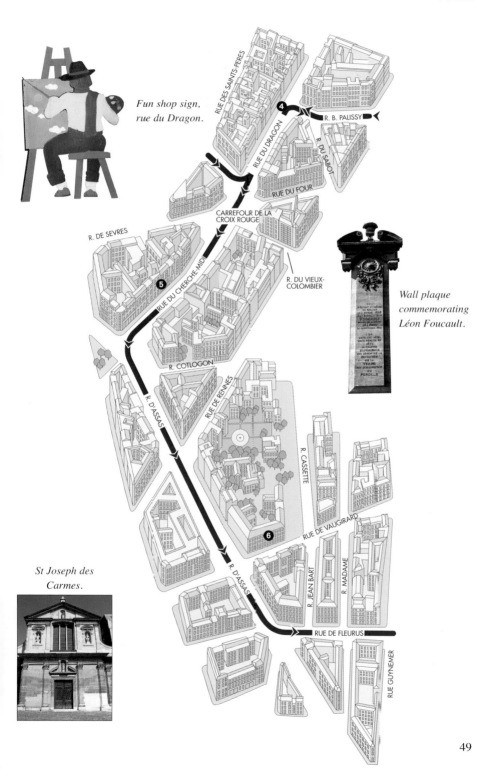

Fun shop sign,
rue du Dragon.

Wall plaque
commemorating
Léon Foucault.

St Joseph des
Carmes.

49

playgrounds, tennis courts, boules, chess, even a bee-keeping school. The garden is sheltered by the **Palais du Luxembourg,** now the seat of the French Senate, built by Marie de Médicis (widow of Henri IV) to remind her of her native Florence. It is also guarded by legions of *gendarmes*, who shoo away tramps and even tidy up stray branches. At weekends, droves of joggers puff their way round the perimeter, while others practise *t'ai chi* and oriental dance, even in extreme weather.

Door carving, No. 14 rue Servandoni.

❼ The **Jardin du Luxembourg** is a sheer delight. At once classically elegant and frothily fun, it is as appealing to lovers as to mothers (it's a perfect place for children). You can retreat to the deep shade of the romantic **Fontaine de Médicis** or the open-air café under the chestnut trees; or sun yourself while watching sailor-suited children playing with model boats in the *grand bassin*; or play a game of chess under the lilac trees. There are statues and flowers, donkey rides, puppet shows, a roundabout,

❽ Rue Servandoni makes an elegant route to St Sulpice, especially at night, when its old-fashioned spherical street lamps are lit. The right medallion on the massive carved door at No. 14 depicts the Florentine Giovanni Servandoni, the principal architect of St Sulpice, unveiling his plan for the church. A little further along is an excellent bistro, run by beetle-browed François, a real character: **Au Bon St Pourçain** (tel. 01 43 54 93 63).

Above and left: in the Jardin du Luxembourg.

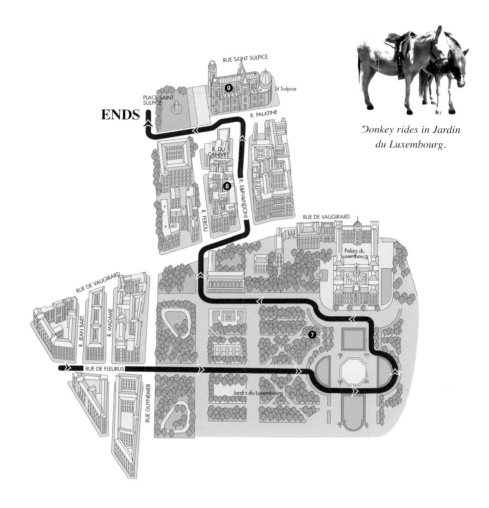

Donkey rides in Jardin du Luxembourg.

9 St Sulpice comes as quite a surprise, looming above a maze of narrow streets. It is enormous, with irritatingly unequal towers (the result of a great deal of meddling by a great many different architects) which mar an otherwise harmonious classical façade. Inside, check out the passionate Delacroix murals in the first chapel on the right, and see if you can spot the bronze meridian line running along the floor of the transept. In **place St Sulpice,** you can admire the imposing **Fontaine des Quatres Evêques** (1844) from **Café de la Mairie,** haunt of students and writers and a good spot for people watching, with branches of **Yves St Laurent** and **Christian Lacroix** comfortably close at hand.

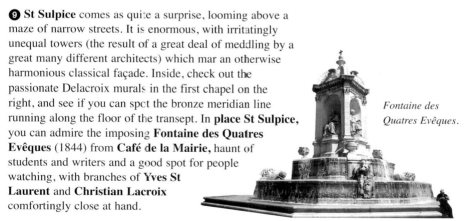

Fontaine des Quatres Evêques.

Secret Gardens and Great Mansions: To Les Invalides

Rodin's The Kiss.

More a wander than a purposeful walk, this Left Bank route leads away from chic St Germain to end at two 'musts': the Rodin Museum and the enormous Invalides complex, a military hospital built by architect Libéral-Bruand at the behest of Louis XIV, The Sun King. Along the way there are charming, little known gardens, grand mansions and the extraordinary shrines of two saints.

Greenery and flowers in square des Mission Etrangers.

A grand entrance in rue de Varenne.

▶ **STARTS**
Junction of rue de Sèvres and rue de Babylone. Nearest metro: Sèvres Babylone.

■ **ENDS**
Avenue de Tourville. Nearest metro: Ecole Militaire, St François Xavier, Varenne.

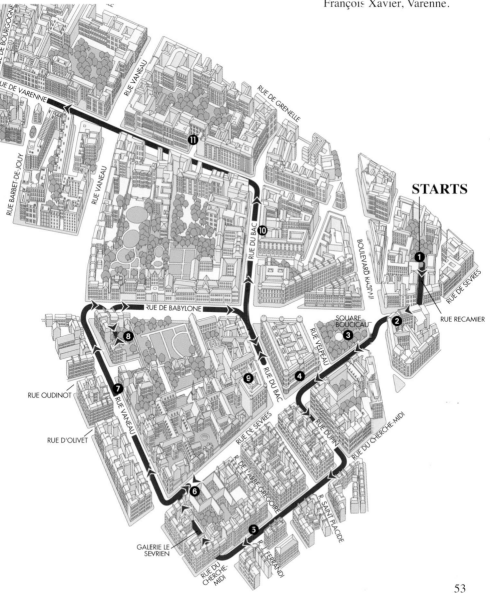

❶ Begin by exploring the first of several quiet open spaces on this walk. **Square Récamier** is a little known sunken garden at the end of rue Récamier. It was named for Madame Julie Récamier, whose beauty was famously matched by her wit. Her sparkling salons, which attracted men of letters such as Hugo, Balzac and Chateaubriand (who was devoted and visited every day) were held close by in rue de la Chaise.

Le Récamier, with its shady outdoor terrace and dignified interior, serves elegant, old-fashioned cuisine and fine Burgundian wines (tel. 01 45 48 86 58).

Square Récamier

❷ If it's time for a cocktail, head for that great ocean liner of a hotel, **Lutétia,** whose mahogany-panelled bar, favoured by literary types, makes a snug place in which to linger. During World War II the hotel made a base for the Gestapo, while after the liberation, it gave shelter to refugees from concentration camps.

Hotel Lutétia.

On Sunday mornings, the excellent **Marché Biologique,** an organic farmers' market, extends along the middle of boulevard Raspail as far as rue de Rennes. Full of the aroma of peaches, cheeses and potato galettes being cooked for instant consumption, this is the only Parisian market where you will find country farmers selling their produce – but don't expect country prices. This is the perfect place to pick up a picnic, to eat later in the Jardin Catherine Labouré or Musée Rodin (see pages 57 and 58).

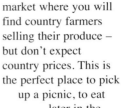

Au Bon Marché.

❸ The garden of **square Boucicaut** affords a momentary respite from the traffic. It commemorates Aristide Boucicaut, whose small 19thC hosiery shop Au Bon Marché, rapidly expanded to become the Left Bank's only department store.

❹ **Au Bon Marché** (French for "good buy" which it no longer is) consists of two iron-framed buildings that were in part designed by Gustave Eiffel. Shop One, with its criss-cross escalators in the centre, makes an elegant setting in which to browse for clothes and household goods. Shop Two, **La Grande Epicérie,** houses a huge range of food, including specialities from Italy, Britain, India and Asia.

❺ **Rue du Cherche-Midi** is packed with little restaurants and bars. Notice, as you pass, a long-established *bûcherie*, a charming 19thC

Delectable peaches, Marché Biologique.

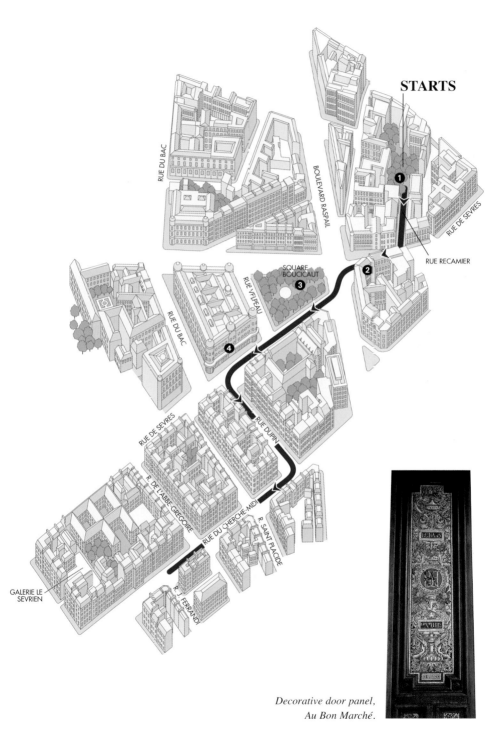

STARTS

RUE DU BAC

BOULEVARD RASPAIL

RUE DE SEVRES

RUE RECAMIER

① ② ③ ④

SQUARE
BOUICAUT

RUE YFIPEAU

RUE DU BAC

RUE DE SEVRES

RUE DUPIN

R. DE L'ABBE GREGOIRE

RUE DU CHERCHE-MIDI

R. SAINT PLACIDE

R. J. FERRAND

GALERIE LE
SEVRIEN

Decorative door panel,
Au Bon Marché.

iron façade for a café, peaceful courtyards, and two lovely 18thC *hôtels particuliers,* Nos. 85 and 87. Run-down No. 85 houses the **Musée Hébert** (closed am and Tues) which displays the works of a now largely forgotten 19thC artist, but it is worth visiting for the atmosphere of this little-changed house with its orginal panelling. Dip into the courtyard of No. 87, now the **Embassy of Mali,** to see its elegant entrance hall and staircase. As a cut-through, and a complete contrast, take the concrete underground galerie le Sevrien opposite, to emerge at rue de Sèvres.

No. 87 rue du Cherche-Midi.

6 Now we come to our walk's first saint, Vincent de Paul, who led a picaresque life of study and adventure before he died in 1660. He was the most prominent churchman in 17thC France, later beatified for his humility and service to others. Together with St Louise de Marillac he founded the Daughters of Charity, confraternities of laywomen dedicated to helping the poor and sick. Glowing red and gold, with stained glass windows depicting scenes from his life, the silent, richly ornamented **Chapel of St Vincent de Paul** was built in 1826. Piled on top of the altar, like an ornament on a wedding cake, is his shrine, made by the silversmith Odiot. A hidden double staircase takes you up; in the shrine lies an eerily realistic wax model of the dead saint.

7 **Rue Vaneau** may look unpromising, but there is rarely nothing of interest in a Paris street. Notice, for example, the charming late 19thC interior of the unspoiled *boulangerie* on the corner of rue Oudinot. Further along at **No. 50,** an ordinary front door reveals a pretty cul-de-sac of little houses, including a shoe-repairer's workshop.

Above and left: at Musée Hébert.

Right: the shrine of St Vincent de Paul.

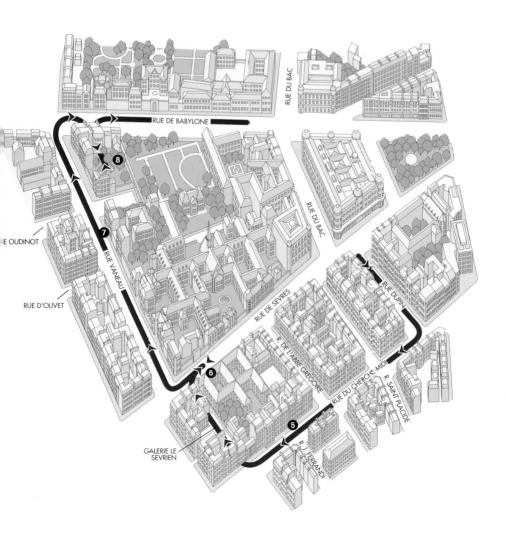

RUE DU BAC

RUE DE BABYLONE

E OUDINOT

RUE VANEAU

RUE D'OLIVET

RUE DU BAC

RUE DE SEVRES

R. DE L'ABBE GREGOIRE

RUE DU CHERCHE-MIDI

RUE DUPIN

R. SAINT PLACIDE

R. J. FERRANDI

GALERIE LE
SEVRIEN

Pumpkins growing in Jardin Catherine Labouré.

❽ The perfect place for your picnic, the walled **Jardin Catherine Labouré** is a quiet and bucolic haven for local residents. It was created on the site of the *potager* (vegetable garden) of the Daughters of Charity of St Vincent de Paul in rue du Bac (see following page). Today there are fruit trees, neat rows of vegetables, a herb garden, an alley of lime trees and vines, as well as a peaceful children's playground.

❾ Catherine Labouré is our walk's second saint, and if you walk round the corner into rue du Bac, (right next to Bon Marché where you started out) her story is revealed in the chapel of **Notre-Dame de la Médaille Miraculeuse.** Catherine was a humble farm girl who had recently joined the Daughters of Charity when, in 1830, she had two apparitions of the Virgin. One of these visions instructed her to have a medal struck which would give its wearers "great graces". Since then, millions of medals have been struck and sold, and the chapel has become a place of pilgrimage, with the shrine of the saint the centre of devotion. Swarms of people gather in this little corner of St Germain, not to shop or eat or look at art, but to fervently pray.

❿ Leave altruism and piety behind and stroll along rue du Babylone, perhaps pausing on the way at **Au Babylone** (tel. 01 45 48 72 13) at No. 13. A family run restaurant with simple food, cramped seating and masses of charm, this place is twice as much fun as many a fancier establishment at a fraction of the cost. (Closed for dinner and Sun lunch.) Now to rue du Bac, a bustling St Germain shopping street, where we find **The Conran Shop,** another friendly little public garden, the **square des Missions Etrangers,** and grand front doors through which you may glimpse elegant private courtyards.

ENDS

⓫ The mood changes as you turn the corner into **rue de Varenne,** positively jam-packed with forbidding, stone-faced mansions. Its gem is **Hôtel Matignon** (No. 57), official residence of the Prime Minister boasting the largest private garden in Paris.

Balzac.

⓬ **Musée Rodin** delightfully combines both mansion and garden. Both the elegant 18thC **Hôtel Biron** (occupied by Rodin from 1908 till his death in 1917) and its fragrant rose-filled gardens display the sculptor's greatest works, such as *The Kiss*, *The Thinker*, *Balzac* and many more. (Closed Mon.)

The Thinker.

Sculptural detail,
Hôtel des Invalides.

13 As you march towards its entrance, the massive yet harmonious façade of **Hôtel des Invalides,** built as a military hospital in 1675, presents an impressive sight, with the glittering, golden Dome church floating behind. Les Invalides contains three military museums: if exhaustion is creeping up, go straight to the second floor, east wing of the **Musée de l'Armée.** Here Napoleon's decline is illustrated: compare the portrait of him as Emperor by Ingres (an overblown, pasty-faced potentate), with the reconstruction of his bedroom on the island of St Helena, including the little canopied camp bed on which he died in 1821. Then make for the **Eglise du Dôme,** a masterpiece of 17thC architecture by Jules Hardouin-Mansart, to see his final resting place. Packed inside six coffins, fitted together like Chinese boxes, Napoleon was laid to rest amid great pomp in 1840. His centrally placed, red porphyry sarcophagus, viewed from a circular gallery, looks fit for a fairytale giant rather than 'The Little Corporal'.

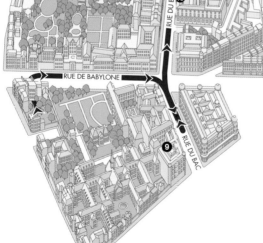

The newly gilded
Eglise du Dôme.

Grand Parade: The Louvre to the Arc de Triomphe

▶ **STARTS**
Place du Palais Royal.
Nearest metro: Palais
Royal/Musée du Louvre.

■ **ENDS**
Arc de Triomphe. Nearest
metro: Charles de Gaulle Etoile.

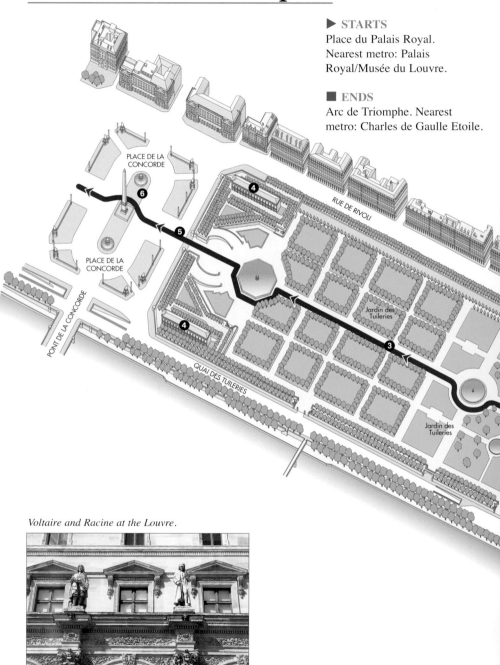

Voltaire and Racine at the Louvre.

For legions of visitors to Paris, this may be the first and very possibly the only walk they take during their stay. Despite the many competing charms of the city, the Champs-Elysées exerts an enormously powerful pull. It forms part of a magnificent axis which begins at the Louvre, and continues through the Jardin des Tuileries and Place de la Concorde, along the avenue des Champs-Elysées to the Arc de Triomphe. It continues on to the Grande Arche de la Défense, which was built in 1989 in the business district on the city's western edge, as part of President Mitterand's *Grands Travaux*.

Mediterranée *by Aristide Maillol, Jardin des Tuileries.*

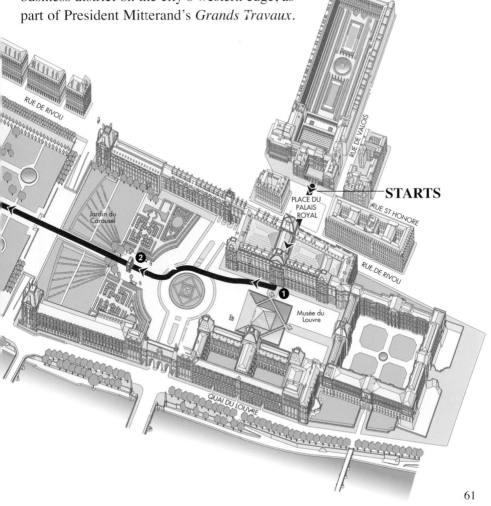

GRAND PARADE: THE LOUVRE TO THE ARC DE TRIOMPHE

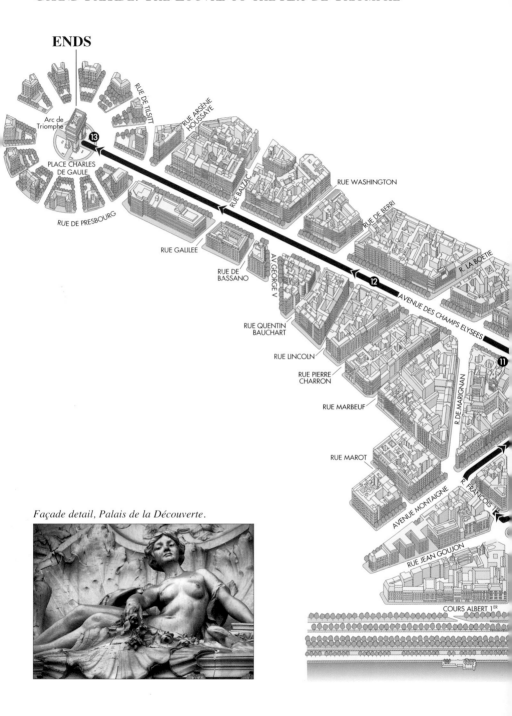

ENDS

RUE DE TILSITT

Arc de Triomphe

PLACE CHARLES DE GAULE

RUE ARSÈNE HOUSSAYE

RUE BALZAC

RUE WASHINGTON

RUE DE BERRI

RUE DE PRESBOURG

RUE GALILÉE

RUE DE BASSANO

AV. GEORGE V

R. LA BOÉTIE

AVENUE DES CHAMPS ELYSEES

RUE QUENTIN BAUCHART

RUE LINCOLN

RUE PIERRE CHARRON

R. DE MARIGNAN

RUE MARBEUF

RUE MAROT

R. FRANÇOIS 1ER

AVENUE MONTAIGNE

RUE JEAN GOUJON

COURS ALBERT 1ER

Façade detail, Palais de la Découverte.

62

This is not a walk, however, for the faint-hearted, especially if you are determined to start by visiting the Louvre and end by climbing the 282 spiral steps to the top of the Arc de Triomphe. In between you must negotiate the traffic and the crowds who come to shop, eat and simply be in the Champs-Elysées. If it gets too much, hop on a metro train or a bus.

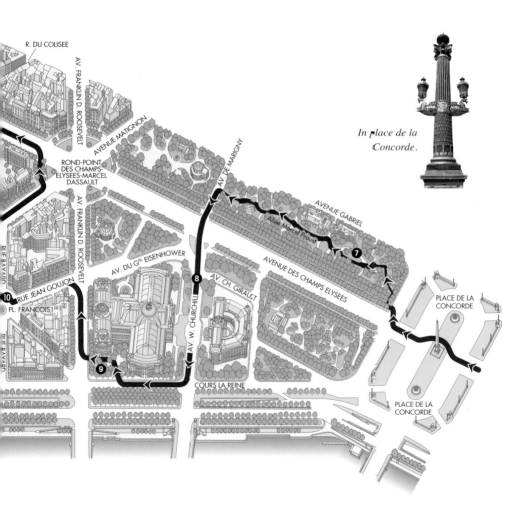

In place de la Concorde.

1 If you are visiting the museum and don't have a Museum Pass or advance ticket (in which case you can enter the fast track at the Richelieu entrance) you should follow signs in the metro to the underground Carousel du Louvre, where the queues are shorter than at the Pyramid entrance.

Human statue: street performer outside the Louvre.

The revamped presentation and layout of the **Musée du Louvre** is superb (pick up a museum plan at the information desk). To get the most from a visit, though, you need an interest in both art and seething humanity. Notably lacking is the hushed, academic atmosphere associated with venerable old museums. This is the Tower of Babel with pictures, plus a dash of the theme park. Like bees to nectar, the tourists are drawn by a system of signposts to the key works. Holy of holies, of course, is the *Mona Lisa* in its thief and fireproof booth, attracting crowds sometimes 20 deep. The room has a curiously festive atmosphere, with bright flags fluttering above tour leaders' heads. Even if you can't properly appreciate the art because of the crowds, pause to take in the dubious sensation of being at a hub of world tourism. Also: arrive early (9am), wear comfortable shoes and be selective about what you choose to see. (Closed Tues.)

Jardin du Carousel

If you are not visiting the museum, emerge from the metro, cross the rue de Rivoli and walk through passage Richelieu towards the Pyramid. To the left and right are the glass-roofed sculpture courts. Suave, snooty **Café Marly,** offering modish, delicate dishes, has ringside seats under the arcades overlooking the Pyramid, with views across the Jardin des Tuileries and of the Eiffel Tower.

2 With the long arms of the Louvre stretched out behind you, proceed in a stately fashion through the graceful **Arc de Triomphe de Carousel,** built to commemorate Napoleonic victories and once topped by the four famed bronze horses from St Mark's in Venice (but returned in 1815). Now the city's grand axis unfolds before your eyes and you can see your goal, the Arc de Triomphe, shimmering in the distance.

Contemporary sculpture in the Jardin des Tuileries.

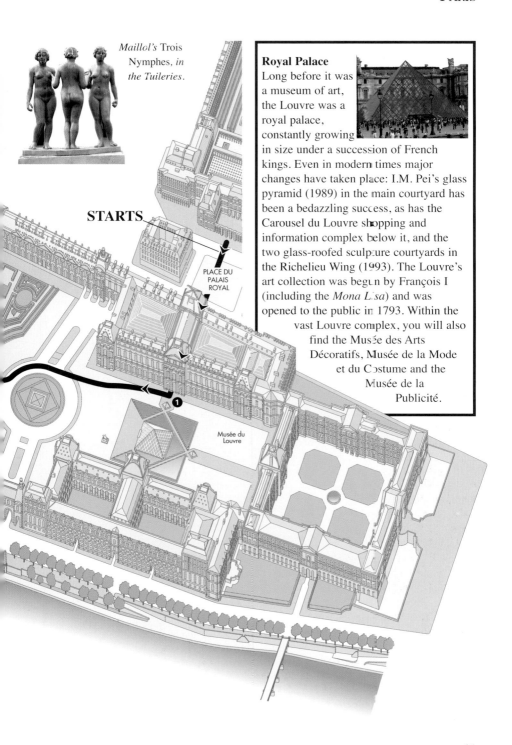

Maillol's Trois Nymphes, *in the Tuileries.*

STARTS

PLACE DU PALAIS ROYAL

Musée du Louvre

Royal Palace
Long before it was a museum of art, the Louvre was a royal palace, constantly growing in size under a succession of French kings. Even in modern times major changes have taken place: I.M. Pei's glass pyramid (1989) in the main courtyard has been a bedazzling success, as has the Carousel du Louvre shopping and information complex below it, and the two glass-roofed sculpture courtyards in the Richelieu Wing (1993). The Louvre's art collection was begun by François I (including the *Mona Lisa*) and was opened to the public in 1793. Within the vast Louvre complex, you will also find the Musée des Arts Décoratifs, Musée de la Mode et du Costume and the Musée de la Publicité.

③ Elegant and formal, with ornamental ponds and terraces, dozens of statues (including 18 bronzes by Aristide Maillol) and wonderful views, the **Jardin des Tuileries** makes a pleasant place in which to stroll. There are cafés under the shade of umbrellas and chestnut trees (good for children, with hamburgers and hot dogs on the menu), donkey rides and toy boats for hire. The garden was laid out by André Le Nôtre, Louis XIV's garden architect, and soon became the place to see and be seen, to show off your beauty or your new carriage. Imagine the Sun King, dressed as a Roman Emperor before 15,000 spectators, in a dazzling equestrian display held here to celebrate the birth of his first son in 1662. At that time a pleasure palace also stood here, built a century earlier by Catherine de Medici. She never lived in it (as her astrologer advised against it), and it was eventually burned down during the Paris Commune of 1871.

The Obelisk.

④ The two pavilions flanking the garden are the **Orangerie,** to your left, and the **Jeu de Paume,** to your right. To visit them, take the ramps on either side of the main path. The Orangerie houses a collection of Monet's *Waterlilies* and other Impressionist paintings, while the Jeu de Paume (originally a real tennis court) displays contemporary art exhibitions.

⑤ Leave the Tuileries by its grandiose gilded gates, framed by Coysevox's two winged horses. Your path into place de la Concorde will be blocked by **La Grande Roue de Paris,** the giant Ferris wheel: perfect for children and marvellous views for all. (Open daily 11am-midnight.)

Hotel Crillon, Place de la Concorde.

⑥ Magnificent and harmonious though it undoubtedly is, **Place de la Concorde,** laid out in the mid-18th century, is all but ruined by the traffic roaring round it (and, for the pedestrian, becomes little more than a danger zone to be traversed). To appreciate it best, head for the middle where splendid vistas open out in all four directions. Here is the perfect focal point, the 3,300 year-old Luxor obelisk which arrived in the 19th century, along with the fountains and statues. Close by stood the guillotine where, during the Revolution, 1,119 people lost their heads, including Louis XVI and Marie Antoinette. On your way round the place, you might take refuge in the famous bar of the unostentatiously luxurious Hotel Crillon.

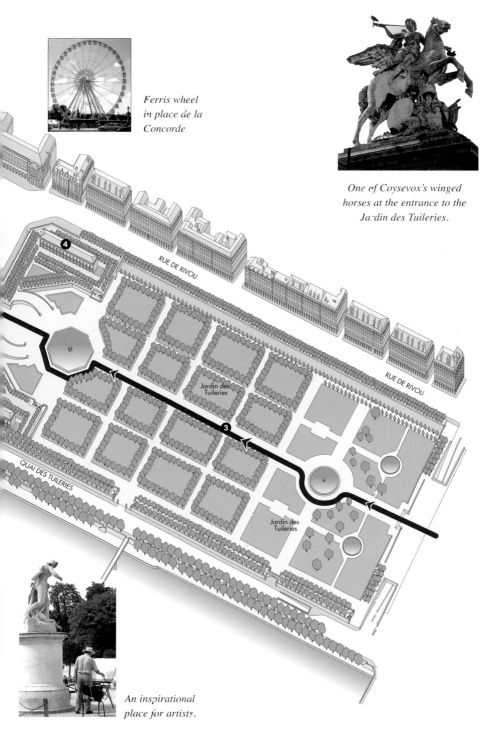

Ferris wheel in place de la Concorde

One of Coysevox's winged horses at the entrance to the Jardin des Tuileries.

RUE DE RIVOLI

RUE DE RIVOLI

Jardin des Tuileries

QUAI DES TUILERIES

Jardin des Tuileries

An inspirational place for artists.

7 Ignore, for a time, the Champs-Elysées (flanked at its entrance by Guillaume Cousteau's rearing *Marly Horses*) and head for the trees on the right, taking the winding path that wanders through the **Jardins des Champs Elysées,** laid out by Jacques Hittorff in 1838. If you are picnicking on this walk, this is the best spot, cosier than the Tuileries, with lush lawns and pretty flowerbeds. The young Marcel Proust played here with Marie de Bernadaky, the model for Gilberte in *A La Recherche du Temps Perdu.*

8 Walking along avenue Winston Churchill, you now enter a part of Paris created for one purpose: the Universal Exhibition of 1900. On either side stand the exuberant **Grand Palais,** adorned by flying horses and chariots at its four corners, and the (only relatively) **Petit Palais,** while ahead lies lovely **Pont Alexandre III.** The glass- and iron-domed and vaulted hall of the Grand Palais can only be glimpsed during visits to the

Petit Palais.

important art exhibitions which are held there. The Petit Palais houses the **Musée des Beaux-Arts de la Ville de Paris,** which has recently been extensively restored, and houses a wide range of art (with 1,300 works on display), spanning from antiquity to the early 20th Century. (Closed Mon.)

Art Nouveau lamp, Pont Alexandre III.

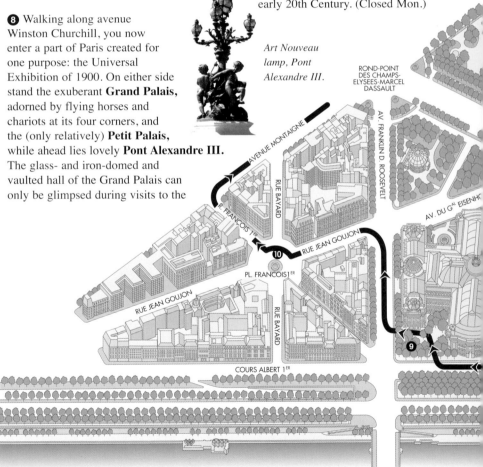

9 Cut through the charming little **Jardin de la Vallée Suisse** – a rocky, watery oasis – to avenue Roosevelt and the **Palais de la Découverte** science museum, with plenty of hands-on exhibits for kids. (Closed Mon.) Opposite is high society restaurant

Decorative panel, Palais de la Découverte.

Lasserre (tel. 01 43 59 53 43), known for its caviar, its ocean-liner decoration, its retractable ceiling and its velvet-lined lift.

10 To get a flavour of this smart, rather solemn district (the 8th *arrondissement*) turn down rue Jean Goujon, passing the luxurious, discreet **Hotel San Régis** and turning into elegant **place François 1er.** In rue Bayard is **Chez Savy,** a venerable bistro serving excellent Auvergnat dishes (avoid the back room; tel. 01 47 23 46 98). As you continue, the sudden presence of Christian Dior announces your arrival in **avenue Montaigne,** once a lugubrious and bandit-infested path known as the allée des Veuves (Widows' Walk) and now the po-faced heart of Parisian *haute couture*.

Chez Savy restaurant.

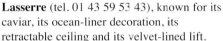

GRAND PARADE: THE LOUVRE TO THE ARC DE TRIOMPHE

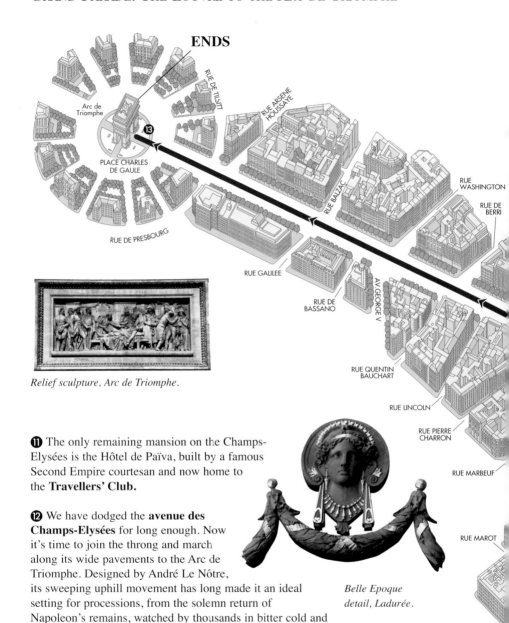

ENDS

Arc de
Triomphe

PLACE CHARLES
DE GAULE

RUE DE PRESBOURG

RUE GALILEE

RUE DE
BASSANO

RUE QUENTIN
BAUCHART

RUE LINCOLN

RUE PIERRE
CHARRON

RUE MARBEUF

RUE MAROT

RUE DE TILSITT

RUE ARSENE
HOUSSAYE

RUE BALZAC

AV. GEORGE V

RUE
WASHINGTON

RUE DE
BERRI

Relief sculpture, Arc de Triomphe.

⓫ The only remaining mansion on the Champs-
Elysées is the Hôtel de Païva, built by a famous
Second Empire courtesan and now home to
the **Travellers' Club.**

⓬ We have dodged the **avenue des
Champs-Elysées** for long enough. Now
it's time to join the throng and march
along its wide pavements to the Arc de
Triomphe. Designed by André Le Nôtre,
its sweeping uphill movement has long made it an ideal
setting for processions, from the solemn return of
Napoleon's remains, watched by thousands in bitter cold and
snow, to the victory parades at the end of World War I and
World War II. Celebrations still take place here every year
on Bastille Day (14 July) and Armistice Day (11
November). On the way, you might pause at a Belle Epoque
café, **Ladurée** or **Le Fouquet's,** and **Virgin Megastore,**
where you can buy tickets for concerts and shows.

*Belle Epoque
detail, Ladurée.*

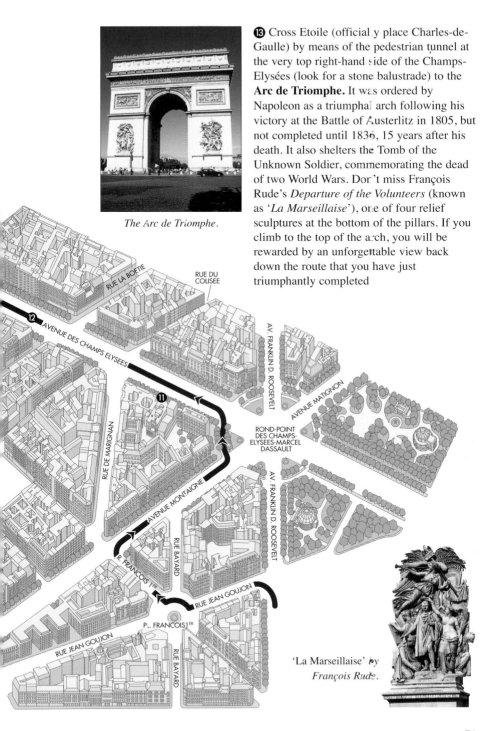

The Arc de Triomphe.

⓭ Cross Etoile (official.y place Charles-de-Gaulle) by means of the pedestrian tunnel at the very top right-hand side of the Champs-Elysées (look for a stone balustrade) to the **Arc de Triomphe.** It was ordered by Napoleon as a triumphal arch following his victory at the Battle of Austerlitz in 1805, but not completed until 1836, 15 years after his death. It also shelters the Tomb of the Unknown Soldier, commemorating the dead of two World Wars. Don't miss François Rude's *Departure of the Volunteers* (known as '*La Marseillaise*'), one of four relief sculptures at the bottom of the pillars. If you climb to the top of the arch, you will be rewarded by an unforgettable view back down the route that you have just triumphantly completed

RUE LA BOETIE

RUE DU COLISEE

12

AVENUE DES CHAMPS ELYSEES

AV. FRANKLIN D. ROOSEVELT

AVENUE MATIGNON

11

ROND-POINT DES CHAMPS-ELYSEES-MARCEL DASSAULT

RUE DE MARIGNAN

AV. FRANKLIN D. ROOSEVELT

AVENUE MONTAIGNE

RUE BAYARD

R. FRANCOIS I ER

RUE JEAN GOUJON

P.. FRANCOIS1 ER

RUE JEAN GOUJON

RUE BAYARD

'La Marseillaise' by
François Rude.

Art and a Park: From the Champs-Elysées to Parc de Monceau

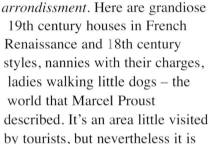

When the draw of the crowds begins to pall, consider turning your back on the pounding Champs-Elysées and taking instead this quiet route through the solid residential streets of the 8th *arrondissment*. Here are grandiose 19th century houses in French Renaissance and 18th century styles, nannies with their charges, ladies walking little dogs – the world that Marcel Proust described. It's an area little visited by tourists, but nevertheless it is studded with unexpected delights, including three jewel-like museums and the poetic Parc de Monceau. Try this route on a weekend: the park is full of happy noise. But, with the business district around the Grands Boulevards closed down, the journey there is much quieter than on weekdays.

Statue in Parc de Monceau.

Palais Elysée guard.

▶ **STARTS**
Avenue des Champs-Elysées at avenue de Marigny. Nearest metro: Champs-Elysées Clemenceau.

■ **ENDS**
Place des Ternes. Nearest metro: Ternes.

Parc de Monceau.

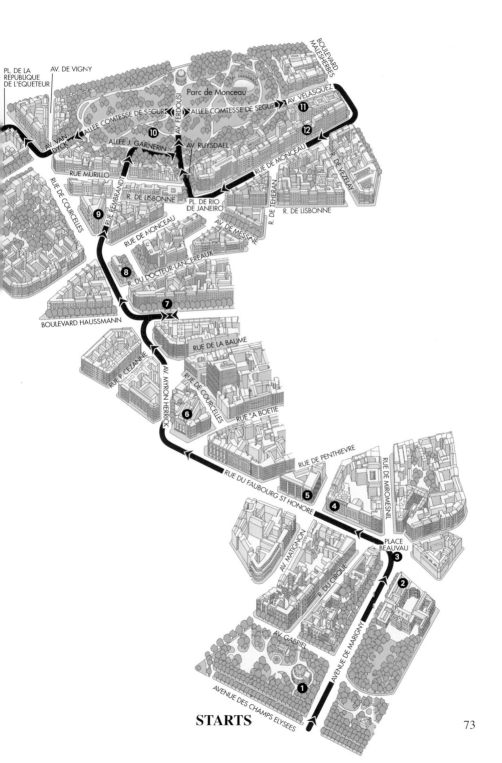

STARTS

Hotel Bristol.

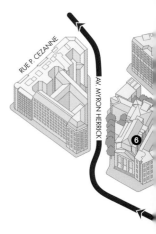

❶ **Théâtre Marigny** was built in 1881 as a panorama rotunda (housing a 360° mural) by Charles Garnier, the architect of the Opéra. It was later converted into a music hall with an open-air foyer, before becoming a standard theatre in the 1920s.

❷ All you can do is catch a glimpse of the elegant **Palais de l'Elysée** behind its high walls and gateway bristling with armed guards. Since 1873 it has been the official residence of the French president, but it was once the home of Madame de Pompadour, (mistress of Louis XV) and the place where Napoleon signed his abdication.

❸ Place Beauvau takes its name from the Marquis de Beauvau, a Marshall of France, who in the 18th century commissioned **Hôtel Beauvau.** The building now houses the Ministry of the Interior, which you can also only glimpse through elegant wrought-iron gates. Notice the **rue des Saussaies** which, strange as it may seem in this urban setting, led to a grove of weeping willows (*saussaie* in French) in the 18th century. During World War II, No. 11 was the headquarters of the Gestapo.

Hôtel Beauvau.

❹ One of the mansions that used to line glossy **rue du Faubourg St Honoré** disappeared in the 1920s to make way for the discreetly opulent **Hotel Bristol,** handy for diplomats and dignitaries visiting the Elysée Palace. The hotel's two highly regarded dining rooms (oak-panelled for winter, glass-walled and overlooking the garden for summer), its intimate bar, silk-hung bedrooms, marble bathrooms and rooftop swimming pool make it perhaps the most luxurious hotel in Paris.

❺ The famous specialist bookshop, **Jullien Cornic,** formerly a local landmark, has sadly closed since our last edition.

❻ As you continue along the rue du Faubourg St Honoré, the flurry of its famous *haute couture* boutiques and art galleries (see page 87) fade away. By the time you arrive at **St Philippe-du-Roule** the street has altogether lost its polish. The neo-classical church around the corner was built in 1784 by Jean-François Chalgrin, better known as the architect of the Arc de Triomphe.

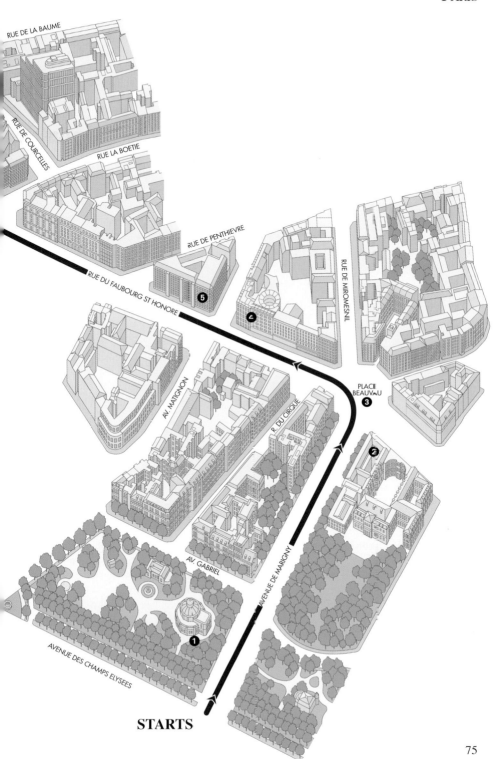

RUE DE LA BAUME

RUE DE COURCELLES

RUE LA BOETIE

RUE DE PENTHIEVRE

RUE DU FAUBOURG ST HONORE

RUE DE MIROMESNIL

PLACE BEAUVAU

AV. MATIGNON

R. DU CIRQUE

AV. GABRIEL

AVENUE DE MARIGNY

AVENUE DES CHAMPS ELYSEES

STARTS

75

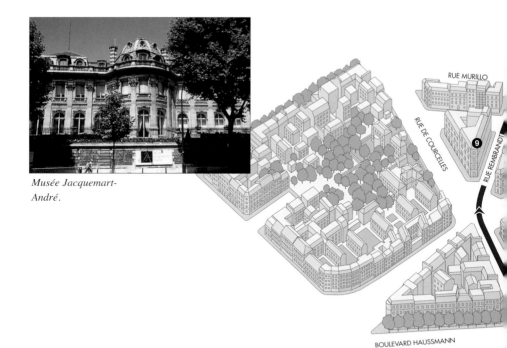

Musée Jacquemart-André.

RUE MURILLO

RUE DE COURCELLES

RUE REMBRANDT

9

BOULEVARD HAUSSMANN

❼ The route now reaches boulevard Haussmann. Constructed in the 1800s, it made a fashionable place for a 19th century millionaire to build an opulent mansion, which is exactly what banker Edouard André did in 1875. He then married a portrait artist (to the surprise of society: she was plain, 40 and of little social standing) called Nélie Jacquemart, and together they set about filling Hôtel André with a staggering collection of art. Nélie left both mansion and contents to the Institut de France and today they are preserved as the **Musée Jacquemart-André** (open daily).

Nélie in particular had the eye of a true connoisseur, and the pair scoured Europe for treasures. They brought back not just paintings and sculpture, but vast tapestries, entire carved doorways, several ceilings and a 30ft wall fresco by Tiepolo. On the ground floor you'll find a glittering circular Grand Salon, a lovely Winter Garden, a double

MUSÉE JACQUEMART ANDRÉ

spiral staircase, and paintings by Rembrandt, Van Dyke, Hals, Boucher and Fragonard. On the first floor the couple installed their Italian collection, including works by Botticelli, Mantegna and Cima di Conegliano. Loveliest of all is the romantic, dreamlike *St George Slaying the Dragon* by Uccello (he slays, she prays). The André's opulent but chaste bedrooms – and the little morning room where they used to meet for breakfast – are also on view.

The Musée Jacquemart-André is one of Paris's most popular art museums. The gracious café in the former dining room with its Tiepolo ceiling and tapestries depicting the *Story of Achilles*, makes a special setting for a light lunch or tea.

Rue de Courcelles.

8 Charlies Dickens wrote of the death of little Paul Dombey at **No. 38 rue de Courcelles** when the writer was living with his family there. After starting *Dombey and Son* in Lausanne, he moved to Paris in November of 1846 and was introduced to France's literary lions – Chateaubriand, Dumas, Lamartine and Hugo.

9 A totally unexpected site greets you at the corner of rue de Courcelles and rue Rembrandt – a red, five-storey Chinese house with pagoda roofs. It was built in 1922 by a Chinese dealer in Asian antiques, Mr Loo. Although he died in 1957, the exclusive **C.T. Loo et Compagnie** still trades here. Follow rue Rembrandt (note **No. 7,** dating from 1900, with its elegant windows and **No. 1,** with its carved wooden front door) towards the enticing greenery of Parc de Monceau (you can enter here by a little gate).

C.T. Loo et Compagnie.

77

⑩ A whimsical, gentle oasis, the little English-style **Parc de Monceau** was originally designed for the Duc d'Orléans by the writer and painter Carmontel in the late 18th century. The strange objects dotted about – columns, obelisks, archways, antique tombs, a semi-circular Corinthian colonnade – are all follies remaining from that time. See if you can also locate the six Belle Epoque monuments of French writers and musicians. In the middle there's an artificial rocky hill, flower-strewn on one side, with a cascade on the other. Swings, a carousel and ice creams for children make this park ideal for family strolls at the weekend.

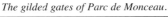

ENDS

⑪ Leave by avenue Velasquez past the small **Musée Cernuschi,** dedicated to Chinese art (with frequent exhibitions). A colourful Milanese financier left this collection, and his fine mansion, to the city of Paris when he died in 1896. The collection traces the development of Chinese art from prehistoric times; perhaps it is best summed up in an evocative 13thC ink and brush drawing of a bird on a twig: humour and simplicity combined with sophistication. (Closed Mon.)

⑫ To reach **Musée Nissim de Camondo,** turn right into boulevard Malesherbes, then right again into rue Monceau. Yet another private collection left to a grateful nation, this 1912 mansion (modelled on the Petit Trianon) is stuffed with 18thC furniture, porcelain, paintings, *objets d'art –* you name it. Its art is an acquired taste, but even if you find it all too much, the place has an undeniable fascination and – best of all – you will have it almost to yourself. It was the

Memorial to a general in avenue Van Dyck.

creation of Moïse de Camondo, a leading Jewish financier, who left the mansion and its contents to the nation in 1935 in memory of his son Nissim, who was killed in World War I. The sense of unreality only lifts when you come across the kitchen – with its 1914 state-of-the-art cast-iron range – the original lift, the bedrooms of Moïse and Nissim (what a tiny bed), and the blue and white tiled bathroom, with all its fittings still in place. A little room next door displays family memorabilia, including poignant photographs of Moïse's daughter, who died in Auschwitz along with her husband and two children. (Closed Mon, Tues.)

The gilded gates of Parc de Monceau.

⑬ Continue along rue Monceau, and then dip briefly back into Parc de Monceau, emerging at avenue Van Dyck. As you leave the park again, take a last look at the magnificent gilded gates and notice **No. 5,** a

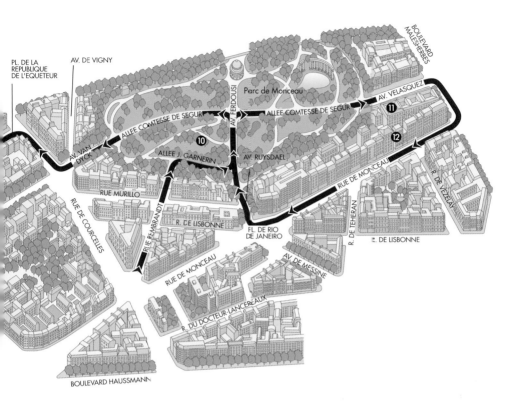

PL. DE LA RÉPUBLIQUE DE L'ÉQUETEUR
AV. DE VIGNY
BOULEVARD MALESHERBES
Parc de Monceau
AV. VELASQUEZ
AV. FERDOUSI
ALLÉE COMTESSE DE SEGUR
ALLÉE COMTESSE DE SEGUR
⑪
⑫
AV. VAN DYCK
⑩
ALLÉE J. GARNERIN
AV. RUYSDAEL
RUE DE MONCEAU
R. DE VÉZELAY
RUE MURILLO
R. DE LISBONNE
R. DE TÉHÉRAN
RUE DE COURCELLES
RUE REMBRANDT
FL. DE RIO DE JANEIRO
R. DE LISBONNE
RUE DE MONCEAU
AV. DE MESSINE
R. DU DOCTEUR-LANCEREAUX
BOULEVARD HAUSSMANN

The Russian Orthodox Cathedral.

neo-Baroque mansion built by chocolate manufacturer Emile Menier. Looking down avenue Hoche you can see the Arc de Triomphe in the distance. Turn right into rue de Courcelles, then left into rue Daru to catch an unexpected sight: the Russian Orthodox **Cathédral St Alexandre Nevsky,** with its five golden domes. It was here in 1921 that Picasso married Olga Khoklova, a dancer with Diaghilev's Ballet Russes. In the streets surrounding the cathedral, Little Russia has grown up, with a restaurant, bookshop, tea shop, school and dance academies.

⑭ **Place des Ternes** is memorable for its gaudy flower stalls and long-established **Brasserie Lorraine.** This place, where stately matrons take tea, serves better than average brasserie food in pleasantly old-fashioned surroundings (tel. 01 56 21 22 00).

Putting on the Ritz: Around the Grands Boulevards

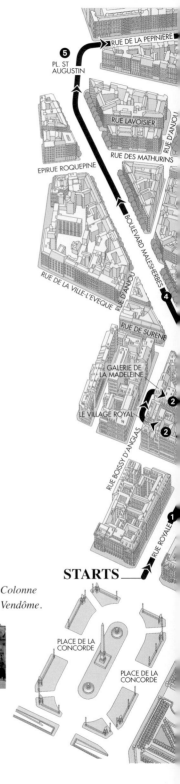

A waft of Chanel seems to hover over these rarefied streets from rue Royale to place Vendôme. The pavements resound to the clip of expensive heels, and the designer-dressed disappear into Cartier, Valentino, Ladurée, Lucas-Carton or the Ritz with a flash of diamonds. These *haute couture* shops, refined restaurants and exclusive hotels might be beyond the means of ordinary mortals. This walk, strictly for window-shoppers, also reveals the part of the city on which Baron Georges-Eugène Haussmann had most impact. Prefect of the Seine under Napoleon III, Haussmann swept away the dirty, cramped Medieval streets, replacing them with a majestic grid of broad avenues and boulevards. When the eight Grands Boulevards linking place de la Madeleine with place de la République opened, their shops and restaurants were the very height of fashion, and the boulevards quickly became places to be seen. By the 19th century the dandies who promenaded here had acquired the name *boulevardiers*. Today, especially at weekends, their wide pavements attract the more dangerous *rollers*, 21st century-crazed rollerbladers.

Colonne Vendôme.

STARTS

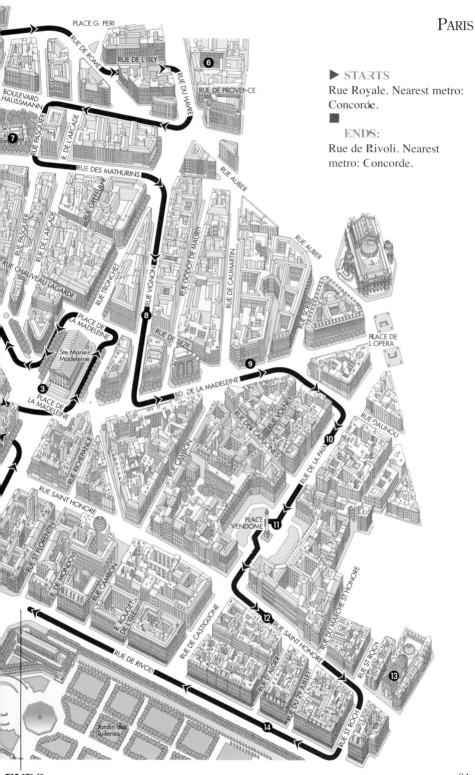

▶ **STARTS**
Rue Royale. Nearest metro:
Concorde.
■
ENDS:
Rue de Rivoli. Nearest
metro: Concorde.

PLACE G. PERI

RUE DE ROME

RUE DE L'ISLY

RUE DU HAVRE

RUE DE PROVENCE

6

7

BOULEVARD
HAUSSMANN

RUE PASQUIER

R. DE L'ARCADE

RUE DES MATHURINS

RUE AUBER

RUE GREFFULHE

RUE AUBER

RUE PASQUIER

RUE DE L'ARCADE

RUE GODOT DE MAURY

RUE TRONCHET

RUE VIGNON

RUE DE CAUMARTIN

RUE SCRIBE

RUE CHAUVEAU LAGARDE

PLACE DE
L'OPERA

PLACE DE
LA MADELEINE

8

RUE DE SEZE

Ste Marie
Madeleine

9

3

PLACE DE
LA MADELEINE

BD. DE LA MADELEINE

RUE VOLNEY

RUE DAUNOU

RUE DES CAPUCINES

10

RUE RICHEPANCE

RUE CAMBON

RUE DE LA PAIX

RUE SAINT HONORE

RUE ST FLORENTIN

R. DE MONDOVI

RUE CAMBON

PLACE
VENDOME **11**

R. ROUGET
DE L'ISLE

RUE DE CASTIGLIONE

RUE SAINT HONORE

12

RUE DU MARCHE ST HONORE

RUE ST ROCH

13

RUE D'ALGER

RUE DU 29 JUILLET

RUE DE RIVOLI

Jardin des
Tuileries

14

RUE ST ROCH

PUTTING ON THE RITZ: AROUND THE GRANDS BOULEVARDS

❶ Rue Royale was laid out in the early 18th century along the line of Louis XIII's – by then defunct – city wall. The architect of place de la Concorde, Jacques-Ange Gabriel, was commissioned to co-ordinate the façades of the grand houses. During the Belle Epoque the street rose to the height of fashion, and the Gucci-clad still flock to its ritzy shops for their jewels (Christofle), china and glass (Bernardoud and Lalique), flowers (Lachaume) and designer children's clothes (Bonpoint). Landmark restaurant and one-time haunt of the glitterati, **Maxim's** is at No. 3, in a house that belonged to Richelieu. Although it has had its heyday, at least put your head round the door to see the superb Art Nouveau decoration. Deliciously gooey cakes arranged in tall cones that defy the laws of gravity are displayed in the window of **Ladurée** (No. 16), an exquisite fin-de-siècle tea room.

❷ The route now takes you through two very different alleys: **Le Village Royal** (Cité Berryer), an open-air enclave of cafés, upmarket boutiques and immaculate buildings (revamped in 1994); and the charmingly old-fashioned **Galerie de la Madeleine,** a covered shopping arcade that has changed little since it was introduced to Paris in the 19th century.

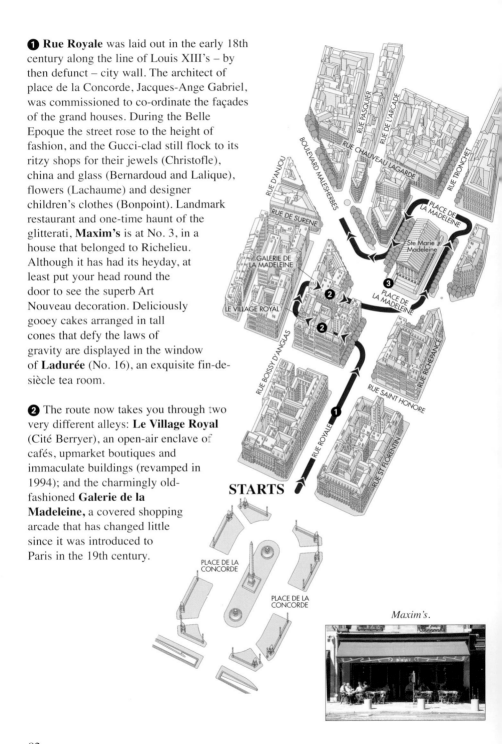

Maxim's.

Neoclassical church of La Madeleine.

Statue, place de la Concorde.

❸ Before you take your life in your hands and cross place de la Madeleine, peek inside **Lucas-Carton** (tel. 01 42 65 22 90). The celebrated restaurant, adorned in spectacular Belle Epoque style by Majorelle, boasts three Michelin stars for the *nouvelle cuisine* of legendary chef Alain Senderens. Dominating the square, the church of Ste-Marie Madeleine (better known as **La Madeleine**), was designed to look like a Roman temple encircled by an impressive Corinthian colonnade. Building began in 1764, but the temple wasn't consecrated until 1842. At one stage it was destined to be a bank, an image it has never quite thrown off, though the lavish marble and gilt interior has an unexpected sensuality and contains some fine sculpture. The best way to see it is to go to one of the many excellent concerts held here. As you come out, look across place de la Concorde to La Madeleine's twin, the Palais Bourbon, a view of perfect symmetry.

Steps on your left lead down to the prettiest **public conveniences** in Paris, decked out in Art Nouveau style by Porcher, with bright tiles, polished mahogany panelling and swirling floral stained glass. Near the entrance, stalls are set up for a mini **flower market**. (Closed Mon.)

A mecca for gourmets, **place de la Madeleine** is known for its epicurean food shops: Caviar Kaspia, La Maison de la Truffe, and arch rivals Hédiard and Fauchon. You can buy anything from beluga caviar to Dom Perignon here – at a price. Don't miss the mouth-watering window displays. An ideal lunch spot, **L'Ecluse** is an animated wine bar with a pretty courtyard (tel. 01 42 65 34 69).

Street lamp, place de la Concorde.

4 As you proceed up **boulevard Malesherbes,** one of Baron Haussmann's broad thoroughfares that radiate from place de la Madeleine, another vista opens up: this time to the imposing Second Empire church of St Augustin. Opulent houses line this boulevard, inhabited in the late-19th century by a bourgeoisie eager to display its wealth. No. 6, for instance, belonged to the Martel brandy family.

Statue of Jeanne d'Arc in place St Augustin.

5 An equestrian statue of a passionate Jeanne d'Arc by Paul Dubois (great-nephew of Pigalle) stands in **place St Augustin** in front of **St Augustin** church (off map).

6 Architect of the Bourse, Brongniart (see page 90) designed a handsome neo-classical Capuchin monastery in 1780. After a spell as a hospital, it was turned into a school, popular with the district's grand residents. A roll-call of the rich and powerful, from Haussmann to Proust, has passed through the hallowed halls of **Lycée Condorcet.** Pop next door to see if there's an interesting exhibition in the cool, light passage which leads to **St Louis d'Antin,** the former monastery's chapel (main entrance on rue Caumartin). The exhibition space has its own little cafeteria. Or, if it's lunchtime and a fine day, buy a sandwich from **Paul,** the Viennese bakery at 55 boulevard Haussmann, and take it to square Louis XVI. To get there, walk along **boulevard Haussmann,** named in memory of the man who changed the face of Paris.

7 A tranquil garden with lush grass, tall trees, and plenty of benches, **square Louis XVI** provides welcome relief from the bustle of the boulevards. But this loveliness masks a grisly past, for this is the site of the Madeleine cemetery, where thousands of victims of the guillotine were buried. The remains of Louis XVI and Marie Antoinette were brought here after their executions and just before Madame Tussaud was smuggled in to take their death masks. When Louis XVIII came to the throne, he had their remains moved to the basilica of St Denis and commissioned Pierre Fontaine to build the **Chapelle Expiatoire** here in their memory. The small circular chapel, now a royalist shrine, contains their statues with the harrowing texts of their last letters engraved beneath them. Reading their final words, you catch a rare glimpse of them as human beings rather than symbols. In the grim little crypt, an altar marks the spot where Louis' body was found. The courtyard tombs are in memory of the Swiss guards killed in the Tuileries attack in 1792. (Open Thurs-Sat 1-5pm.)

8 Food's the thing in **rue Vignon** where **La Maison du Miel** at No. 24 sells a huge range of honey varieties: thyme, lavender, eucalyptus to name but a few. Close by is **Duo Trio,** a shop specialising in tea and chocolate – a perfect place for presents.

La Maison du Miel in rue Vignon.

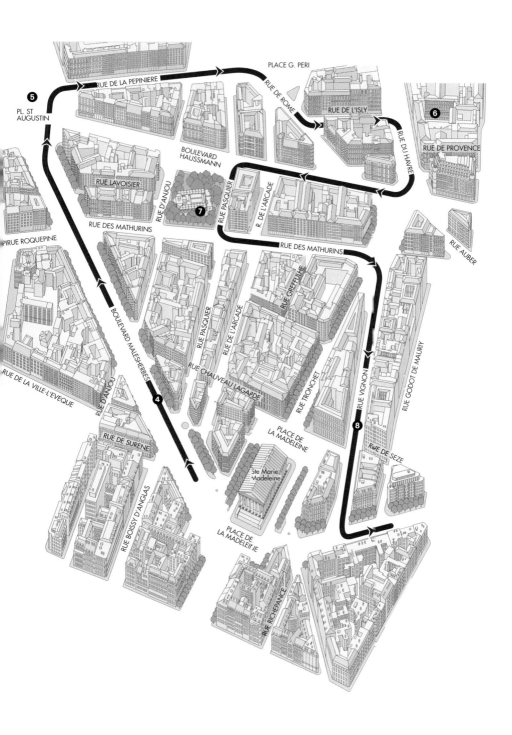

9 In boulevard des Capucines, Edith Piaf, Yves Montand and the Beatles performed at the **Olympia** (No. 28), still a top showbiz venue. Further on at No. 39, **Musée Fragonard** is a jewel of a museum dedicated to perfume. Concerned with the industry as well as the end product, the museum's displays range from ancient stills to beautiful Limoges bottles and paintings of ladies at their toilette. (Closed Mon. See page 95.)

Olympia concert hall.

10 Turn down rue Daunou, where the American community hangs out at **Harry's Bar** (at the far end of the street, No.5). In 1806 the church of a Capuchine convent was destroyed to make way for **rue de la Paix,** which soon attracted the city's most elegant *haute couture* houses and jewellers. By the end of the 19th century it had become Paris' most stylish shopping street. Many of the big names are still here, including Cartier.

Figures outside the restaurant American Dream in rue Daunou.

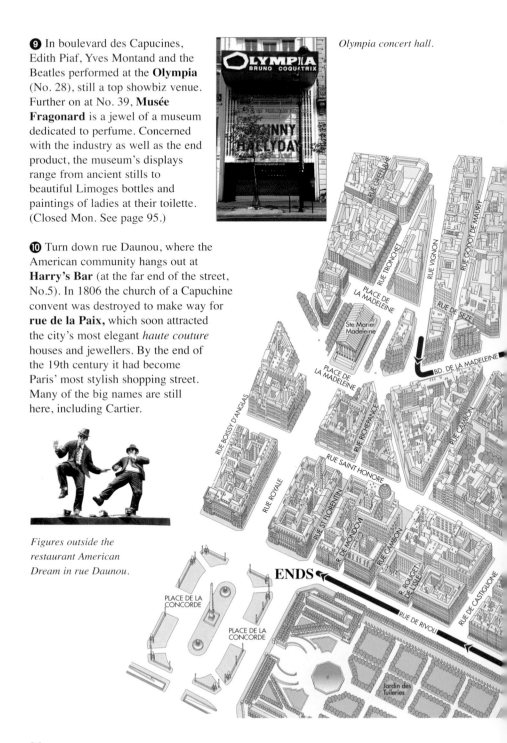

⓫ Even the air in **place Vendôme** seems different – scented by fragrances emanating from its many *parfumeries*. Built under Louis XIV by Jules Hardouin-Mansart, it has an untouchable, opulent beauty, ringed by perfectly proportioned 17thC buildings. These are now occupied by smart shops such as Bulgari and, arguably the most famous hotel in the world, **The Ritz** at No. 15. The square is dominated by the **Colonne Vendôme,** surmounted by a statue of Napoleon in Roman dress. Modelled on Trajan's column in Rome, it is covered with a spiral of friezes depicting episodes from the Battle of Austerlitz in bronze melted down from enemy cannon.

Place Vendôme.

⓬ Everything the well-heeled need to equip themselves can be bought at the refined shops crowded into the glossy thoroughfares of **rue St Honoré** and its extension **rue Faubourg-St Honoré.** Here you will encounter fashion's *grandes dames* and important newcomers; first Guerlain, Goyard, Gucci and further west Escada, Hermès, Lanvin, Givenchy, Valentino, Dior, Ferragamo, J.P. Todd and Versace. **215 St Honoré** is a great stopping point for a delicious sandwich, and gets very busy at lunchtime with locals.

⓭ Bullet holes still pepper the façade of the church of **St Roch** from a battle between Napoleon's Republican forces and royalist troops fought here just days before his promotion to commander-in-chief in 1795. A cavernous building by Lemercier (who built the Louvre) it is a treasure trove of art, including Vien's *St Denis Preaching to the Gauls*. Corneille, the playwright; Le Nôtre, the gardener; and Diderot, the philosopher, are buried here.

⓮ Created between 1800 and 1835 for promenading, **rue de Rivoli** is, at this point, an elegant uniform colonnade. Inset with shops; among them, long-established Anglo-French bookshop, **Galignani** (No. 224); genteel tea room, **Angelina** (No. 226); luxurious **Hôtel Meurice** (No. 228); and an outpost of the British **W.H. Smith** (No. 248).

Commerce and Culture: From the Bourse to the Opéra

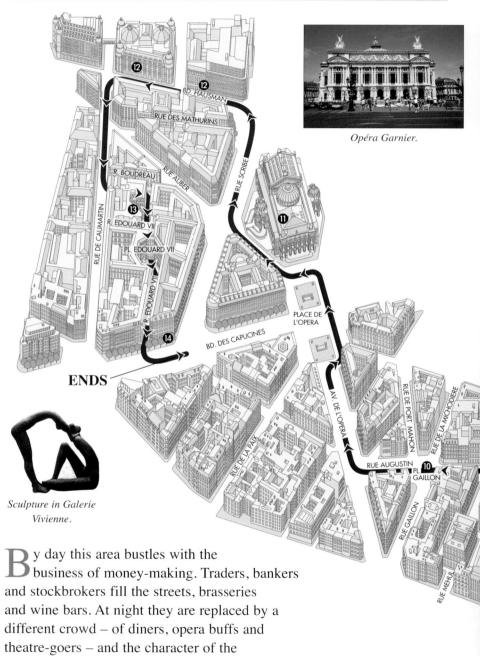

Opéra Garnier.

BD. HAUSMAN

RUE DES MATHURINS

R. BOUDRÉAU

RUE AUBER

RUE SCRIBE

RUE DE CAUMARTIN

R. EDOUARD VII

PL. EDOUARD VII

R. EDOUARD VII

PLACE DE L'OPÉRA

BD. DES CAPUCINES

ENDS

AV. DE L'OPÉRA

RUE DE LA PAIX

RUE DE PORT MAHON

RUE DE LA MICHODIÈRE

RUE AUGUSTIN

PL. GAILLON

RUE GAILLON

RUE MEHUL

Sculpture in Galerie Vivienne.

B y day this area bustles with the business of money-making. Traders, bankers and stockbrokers fill the streets, brasseries and wine bars. At night they are replaced by a different crowd – of diners, opera buffs and theatre-goers – and the character of the neighbourhood changes. This walk connects the

▶

STARTS
Rue du Quatre Septembre.
Nearest Metro: Bourse.

■

ENDS
Boulevard des Capucines.
Nearest Metro: Opéra.

Sentinel at the Palais de la Bourse.

streets of a district that owes much to Baron Haussmann's grand plan to open up the city. Monuments to bygone fortunes and vast impressive buildings compete for attention, all the way from the Palais de la Bourse to the Hôtel Scribe by way of the Hôtel du Crédit Lyonnais, Bibliothèque Nationale, Opéra Garnier and the Grands Magasins. Older than most of their grand neighbours are the charming little *passages* – some almost frozen in time. These few survivors of Haussmann's wholesale demolition are a fascinating slice of city history.

STARTS

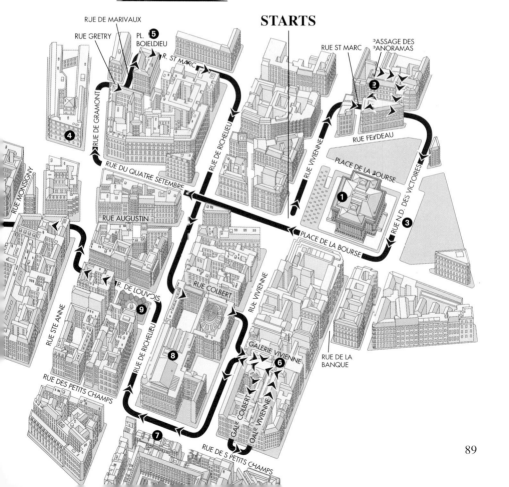

COMMERCE AND CULTURE: FROM THE BOURSE TO THE OPERA

❶ Stand at the junction of rues Vivienne and de la Bourse for the best view of Alexandre Théodore Brongniart's eloquent Grecian **Palais de la Bourse,** commissioned by Napoleon as a Temple to Commerce,

Palais de la Bourse.

Sign outside Le Vaudeville brasserie.

and built on the site of a convent. Although the Stock Exchange left in 1987, the trading floor is still occupied by the futures and traded options markets. You can only witness capitalism at work here on an organized tour (tel. 01 49 27 55 50). As you continue up **rue Vivienne,** the heaving 1925 brasserie **Le Vaudeville** (tel. 01 40 20 04 62) occupies the corner at No. 29. Decked out with marble and mirrors, it's particularly lively at lunchtime with parties of ebullient traders.

❷ The epitome of fashion in the early 19th century, pedestrian shopping arcades concentrated a variety of smart shops and tea rooms under one vaulted glass roof, making shopping sociable and easy, and protecting shoppers from the rain. Perhaps the most famous, the **Passage des Panoramas** boasted an added attraction in American Robert Fulton's revolving 'panoramas', a precursor to the movies. Enter the passage from rue St Marc and explore it and its warren of

Shop sign in the Passage des Panoramas.

interconnecting arcades: Galeries St Marc, des Variétés, Montmartre and Feydeau. Despite the diversity of their little shops, all retain their 19thC character. In the passage, you'll find shops selling second-hand books, stamps, stationery, pictures, furniture, clothes and toys, as well as tea rooms and restaurants. **L'Arbre à Canelle** (No. 57; tel. 01 43 31 68 31), is worth a visit for its eye-catching pastoral decoration.

You could extend this part of the walk from the end of this passage by crossing boulevard Montmartre (off map) to **Musée Grévin** (a waxworks museum) and the charming **Passage Jouffroy,** a continuation of Passage des Panoramas. This arcade eventually links with **Passage Verdeau.**

Musée Grévin.

STARTS

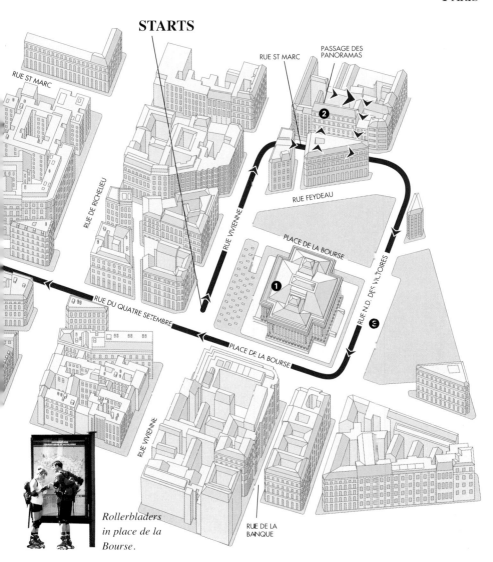

RUE ST MARC

RUE DE RICHELIEU

RUE ST MARC

PASSAGE DES PANORAMAS

❷

RUE VIVIENNE

RUE FEYDEAU

PLACE DE LA BOURSE

❶

RUE N.D. DES VICTOIRES

❸

RUE DU QUATRE SEPTEMBRE

PLACE DE LA BOURSE

RUE VIVIENNE

Rollerbladers in place de la Bourse.

RUE DE LA BANQUE

❸ Restaurants in **rue Notre Dame des Victoires** cater to different tastes and pockets. The area gets extremely busy around lunchtime, with financial bigwigs putting their deals on hold while they eat out. At No. 40 the traditional brasserie **Gallopin** (tel. 01 42 36 45 38), founded in 1876, serves simple fare in friendly style.

Rue des Colonnes.

❹ Follow the route along rue du Quatre Septembre, past the attractive arcades of the late-18thC **rue des Colonnes.** Turn right up rue Gramont beside **Hôtel du Crédit Lyonnais,** a monumental late-19thC building, for which Gustave Eiffel designed an iron frame.

91

❺ The spot from which to gaze on the elaborate 19thC façade of the **Opéra Comique** is place Boieldieu. Also known as Salle Favart, after the 18thC playwright and director of the Italian troupe who introduced *opéra comique* to Paris, it is still the principal venue for light opera and operetta. Built on the site of the former Théâtre des Italiens (a grand complex owned by the Duc de Choiseul) the opera burned down twice in the 19th century. The current building by Bernier dates from 1894-8.

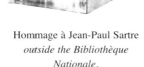

Hommage à Jean-Paul Sartre *outside the Bibliothèque Nationale.*

❻ With its fine mosaic floor and moulded arcade of alluring shops, **Galerie Vivienne** is one of the most delightful of the city's *passages*. It was built later than most in 1923 by F.J. Delannoy, and like the others, its specialist boutiques cater to both mundane and esoteric needs. Step inside and turn right for the painted, classical-style **Galerie Colbert,** with exhibition spaces, an Institute of further education, and a tempting bookshop. Its restaurant, **Le Grand Colbert,** is a perfect Belle Epoque replica with a profusion of palms but a tourist clientele. If you need a break, in Galerie Vivienne **A Priori Thé** is an appealing *salon de thé* at Nos 35-37. Peek through the glass at No. 13 for a glimpse of a fine wrought-iron staircase leading to apartments where convict-turned-crime-buster François Vidocq lived in 1840.

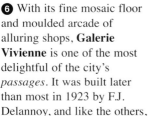

Galerie Colbert.

❼ In rue des Petits-Champs, don't miss **Willi's Wine Bar** (tel. 01 42 61 05 09), 25-year-old venture of Brit Mark Williamson, who takes his vintages seriously and keeps an enviable cellar. The sophisticated ambience and excellent food draw the city slickers.

❽ Cardinal Mazarin created the massive building that is now the **Bibliothèque Nationale** in the 17th century by combining two of his mansions, the Hôtels Tubeuf and Chivry. Although split up after Mazarin's death, part of the complex became the repository of the royal library. Over the years the library evolved into one of the finest collections of books, manuscripts, maps, prints and medallions in the world. Since 1537, a copy of every book published in France has, by law, been kept here. In 2000, when the library relocated to a new building at Tolbiac (one of Mitterand's monuments), some 10,000,000 books, periodicals and recordings were moved. Today you can view the medallion, coin and jewellery collection in the **Musée du Cabinet des Médailles et des Antiques;** the temporary exhibitions in the **Mansart** and **Mazarin** galleries and **Rotonde Colbert** photo gallery; and – through glass – Henri Labrouste's ravishing Second Empire round **reading room.**

❾ **Square Louvois** was not always so peaceful. Louvel, an anti-Bourbon fanatic, assassinated the Duc de Berry here in 1820 during a performance of the *Carnival of Venice* at a *salle d'opéra* on this site. Louvel was arrested and guillotined, while the King had the theatre demolished. The square and its exuberant Visconti fountain, **Fontaine Louvois,** recall one of Louis XIV's ministers, whose palatial townhouse was nearby.

Visconti fountain in square Louvois.

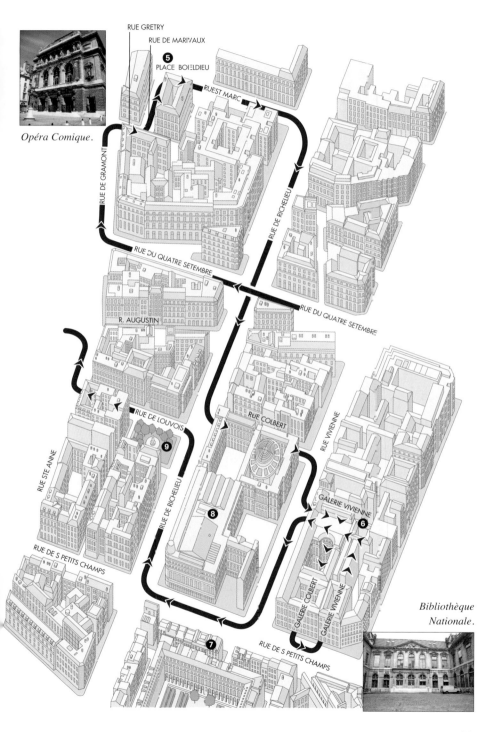

RUE GRETRY

RUE DE MARIVAUX

⑤ PLACE BOIELDIEU

RUE ST MARC

RUE DE GRAMONT

RUE DE RICHELIEU

Opéra Comique.

RUE DU QUATRE SETEMBRE

R. AUGUSTIN

RUE DU QUATRE SETEMBRE

RUE DE LOUVOIS

RUE COLBERT

RUE VIVIENNE

RUE STE ANNE

⑨

RUE DE RICHELIEU

⑧

GALERIE VIVIENNE

⑥

RUE DE S PETITS CHAMPS

GALERIE COLBERT

GALERIE VIVIENNE

*Bibliothèque
Nationale.*

⑦

RUE DE S PETITS CHAMPS

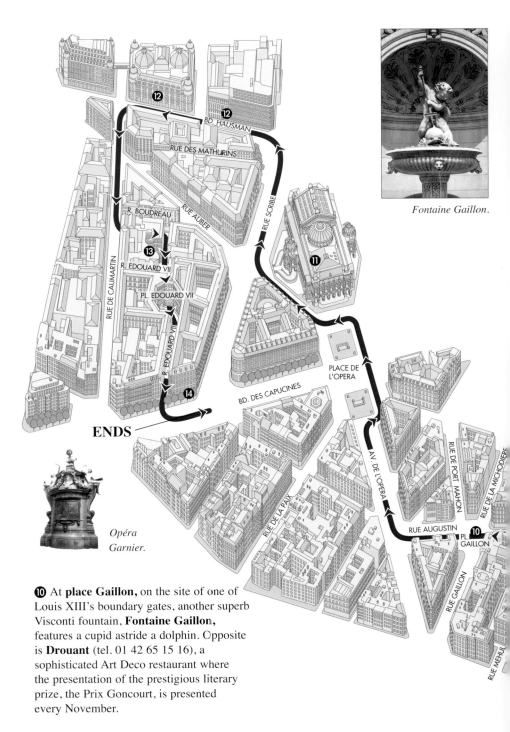

Fontaine Gaillon.

ENDS

Opéra Garnier.

10 At **place Gaillon,** on the site of one of Louis XIII's boundary gates, another superb Visconti fountain, **Fontaine Gaillon,** features a cupid astride a dolphin. Opposite is **Drouant** (tel. 01 42 65 15 16), a sophisticated Art Deco restaurant where the presentation of the prestigious literary prize, the Prix Goncourt, is presented every November.

11 As you reach the top of avenue de l'Opéra, on the left you will see the ever-popular **Café de la Paix,** which has preserved its 19thC decoration by Charles Garnier. Take a table outside if you want to watch the world go by. The building

Galeries Lafayette.

that most personifies the opulence of the Second Empire, **Opéra Garnier,** emerged from its millennium facelift even more dazzling than before. A cornucopia of columns, friezes, gilded figures and busts decorate the ornate façade, lending it an air of irresistible joy. Go inside to see the magnificent white-marble double staircase, and (on a tour or at a performance only) the plush red velvet and gold auditorium, with Chagall's 1960s domed ceiling – the only jarring note. What used to be the emperor's private entrance now leads to a museum containing scores, models of sets and memorabilia including Nijinsky's ballet shoes.

12 With the increasing prosperity of the bourgeoisie in the early 20th century, suitable shops had to be built to cater for their needs. Grands Magasins – emporiums such as **Galeries Lafayette** and **Au Printemps** – are the result. In striking Belle Epoque buildings stretching for several blocks in boulevard Haussmann, these department stores contain acres of floor space devoted to their huge selections of fashion, household goods, jewellery, perfume and cosmetics.

13 Flamboyant, Art Nouveau **Théâtre de l'Athenée Louis Jouvet** and its tucked-away square, **square de l'Opéra Louis Jouvet,** are named in memory of the theatre's most celebrated actor-director. The statue in the middle of the square, *Poet riding Pegasus*, is a monument to Victor Hugo by Alexandre Falguière. **Place Edouard VII** also sports a theatre and a statue, a representation by Paul Landowski of this English king on horseback.

Statue of Edward VII

14 **14 boulevard des Capucines** was the scene of the Lumière brothers' first public projection of animated photography with the help of their invention, the cinematograph, on 28 December 1895. Next door, **Hôtel Scribe** (1 rue Scribe), a vast Second Empire pile, was the press HQ of the allied forces during World War II. Further up rue Scribe, **Musée Fragonard** (No. 9), is a perfume museum in a lovely wood-floored house where you can view stills, copper decanters, pipettes, soap moulds, 18thC scent bottles and potpourri.

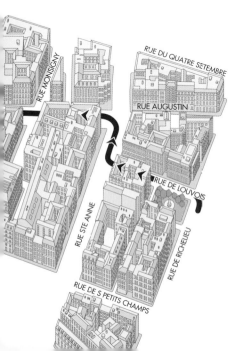

RUE DU QUATRE SETEMBRE
RUE MONSIGNY
RUE AUGUSTIN
RUE DE LOUVOIS
RUE STE ANNE
RUE DE RICHELIEU
RUE DES PETITS CHAMPS

From the Sublime to the Surreal: Palais Royal to Beaubourg

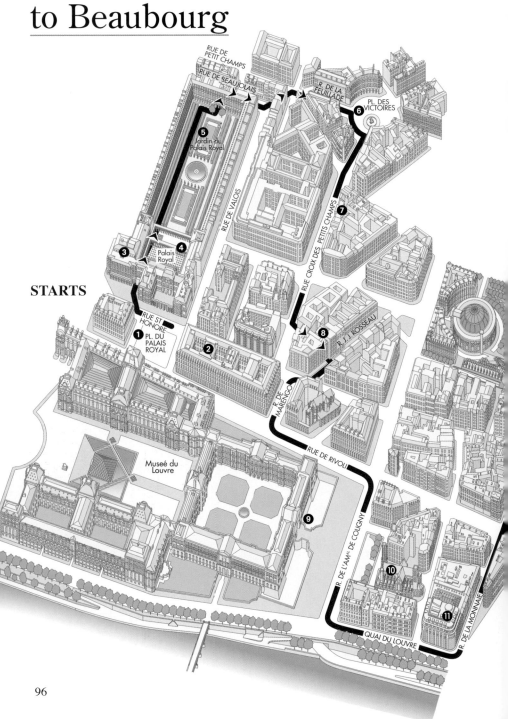

RUE DE PETIT CHAMPS

RUE DE BEAUJOLAIS

R. DE LA FEUILLADE

PL. DES VICTOIRES ❻

❺ Jardin du Palais Royal

RUE DE VALOIS

RUE CROIX DES PETITS CHAMPS

❼

STARTS

❸ ❹ Palais Royal

R. J. J. ROSSEAU

RUE ST HONORÉ

❶ PL. DU PALAIS ROYAL

❷

❽

R. DE MARENGO

Museé du Louvre

RUE DE RIVOLI

❾

R. DE L'AML DE COLIGNY

❿

R. DE LA MONNAIE

⓫

QUAI DU LOUVRE

► **STARTS**
Place du Palais Royal.
Nearest metro: Palais Royal.

■ **ENDS**
Pompidou Centre. Nearest
metro: Châtelet, Rambuteau.

*Metro station
detail.*

A walk of contrasts, this route begins peacefully in a refined 18thC garden and ends in hurly-burly and happy confusion, bang in the present day at Les Halles and the Pompidou Centre, known to all as Beaubourg. Along the way, meet the Sun King, find a perfectly preserved 19thC shopping arcade, remember a monstrous massacre and see all Paris laid at your feet from a little known vantage point – none of the queues of the Eiffel Tower, right in the middle of the city and free.

Au Pied de Cochon.

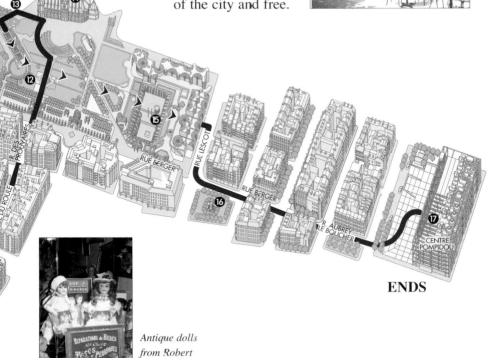

ENDS

*Antique dolls
from Robert
Capia.*

Cour d'Honneur, Palais Royal.

❶ The tarmac expanse of the place du Palais Royal is a popular spot for rollerbladers, young and old, expert and wobbly, where at weekends they wheel about in front of the **Palais Royal.** Much rebuilt, and now housing the *Conseil d'Etat*, it was built by Cardinal Richelieu for himself. He willed it to the Crown and it became the childhood home of Louis XIV.

❷ Housed in a former department store, the **Louvre des Antiquaires** is a peaceful and very expensive shopping mall entirely devoted to antiques, art and *objets d'art*. Strictly no bargains. (Closed Mon.)

❸ The foyer of the **Comédie Française** displays the chair in which Molière collapsed and died during a performance of his play, entitled – ironically – *The Hypochondriac*. The works of the great French playwright are still performed here.

❹ Walk through the arches between Comédie Française and Palais Royal and you will find yourself, bizarrely, amongst a sea of striped stumps. Some tall, some short, these columns have blighted the **Cour d'Honneur** of the Palais Royal since 1986, when President Mitterand's flamboyant arts minister, Jack Lang, commissioned the work from sculptor Daniel Buren. The cylinders are good for resting on, and for rollerblading around, but it's quite hard to see the artistic point.

❺ Today it's hard to believe that the **Jardin du Palais Royal** was once a denizen of vice, its arcades filled with bordellos and gambling dens. Enclosed – in the 1780s – by uniform, arcaded houses, the garden is the most intimate and elegant open space in Paris, lined by shady avenues of limes. There are unusual shops in the arcades, temporary sculptures, shady cafés, and the romantic and long-famous restaurant, **Le Grand Véfour** (tel. 01 42 96 56 27). Here Napoleon courted Josephine, and the novelist Colette, who lived almost next door at **No. 9 rue de Beaujolais,** was a regular. She could often be seen writing at her windows overlooking the garden.

Contemporary sculpture, Jardin du Palais Royal.

Jardin du Palais Royal.

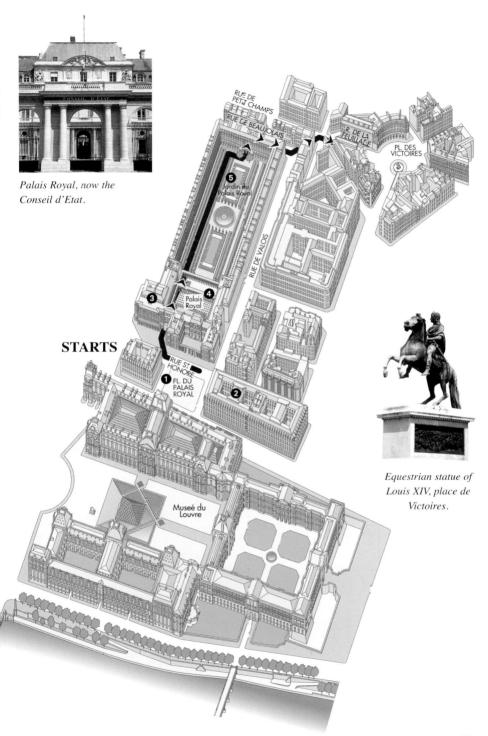

Palais Royal, now the
Conseil d'Etat.

RUE DE
PETIT CHAMPS

RUE DE BEAUJOLAIS

R. DE LA
FEUILLADE

PL. DES
VICTOIRES

❺
Jardin du
Palais Royal

RUE DE VALOIS

❸ Palais ❹
Royal

STARTS

RUE ST
HONORÉ

❶ PL. DU
PALAIS
ROYAL

❷

Equestrian statue of
Louis XIV, place de
Victoires.

Museé du
Louvre

6 Walking along Rue des Petits Champs (see page 92) notice the minute **passage des Deux Pavillons** on the right. Ahead, Louis XIV rears up on his horse, dominating **place des Victoires.** This equestrian statue of 1822 was a replacement for the original – an over-the-top gold affair surrounded by burning torches, erected during the reign of the Sun King by the sychophantic Duc de La Feuillade on his own land. He then commissioned the architect Hardouin-Mansart to create a suitable setting: the circular *place*. The original statue was an obvious target for the mobs of the Revolution. Today its big-wigged replacement is surrounded by expensive designer boutiques such as Thierry Mugler and Kenzo.

7 Rue Croix des Petits Champs skirts the massive **Banque de France,** founded by Napoleon. Built by François Mansart, but much changed, in the early 18th century it was the home of the Comte de Toulouse, son of Louis XIV and Madame de Montespan. Behind today's dull 19thC façade (the only original section, along rue Vrillière, can be seen from place des Victoires) lies the Comte's sumptuous 50m-long Galerie Dorée, sadly closed to the public.

8 Beautiful **galerie Véro-Dodat** has been frozen in time since it opened in 1826. It was named after the two butchers who built the arcade, installing the first gas lighting in Paris. No. 26 used to house the famous purveyor of antique dolls, Robert Capia.

9 Crossing rue de Rivoli and approaching the Seine, admire the majestic **Colonnade de Perrault,** which forms the east wing of the Louvre (see page 64). Dating from 1668, this facade is a textbook example of French classical architecture and was designed by Claude Perrault, brother of the writer of fairy tales, Charles.

10 The flurry of Gothic architecture across the road announces **St Germain l'Auxerrois,** the parish church to the Louvre when it was occupied by the royal court. The bell here began tolling at midnight on 24 August 1572 to signal the start of the St Bartholomew's Day Massacre, during which 3000 Protestants, in town for the wedding of Henri de Navarre and Marguerite de Valois, were killed in their beds. After seeing the church, you could refresh yourself in the elegant, century-old *salon de thé,* **Patisserie St Germain l'Auxerrois,** on the corner.

Rue de Rivoli.

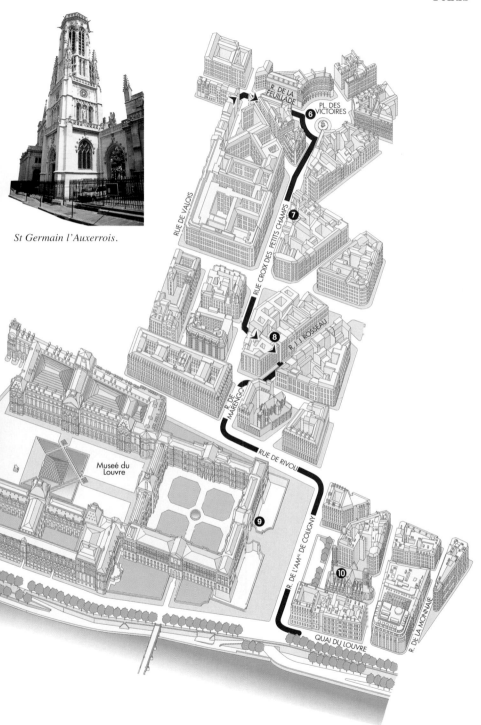

St Germain l'Auxerrois.

⓫ The sprawling low-price department store **La Samaritaine** has a wonderful (free) plus: take the lift to the 9th floor (where there is a café) and walk up the spiral stairs to the open-air Panorama where all Paris is laid before you (closed Nov-Apr). An old ceramic legend locates points of interest. The store was undergoing extensive renovation when we went to press.

⓬ Your surroundings become decidedly tackier as you move towards the looming St Eustache, but the shady, watery **Jardin des Halles** provides some relief and a fine view of the Bourse du Commerce (Commodities Exchange).

⓭ Au Pied de Cochon is a vestige of Les Halles when it was the city's central food market (now moved to the suburbs) and known as 'the belly of Paris'. Then as now the brasserie is open 24 hours a day, but the signature *gratinée aux oignons* and pigs' trotters are disappointing; the shellfish is a better bet (tel. 01 40 13 77 00).

⓮ With its Gothic ground plan, neo-classical façade and Renaissance interior, the church of **St Eustache,** second only in size to Notre-Dame, has great majesty and a soaring elegance.

⓯ Plunge into the subterranean **Forum des Halles** shopping and leisure complex through Porte du Jour, following the blue signs for Porte Lescot. Beneath the Forum, in a sort of inverted pyramid, lies the world's largest underground station, Châtelet-Les Halles.

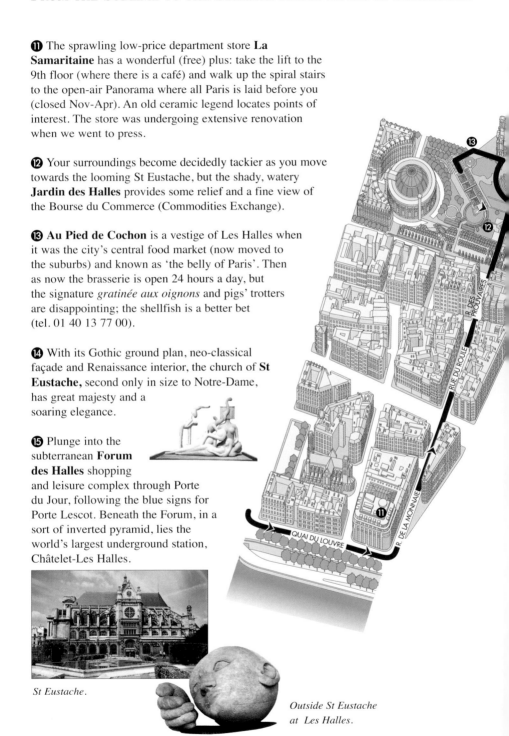

St Eustache.

Outside St Eustache at Les Halles.

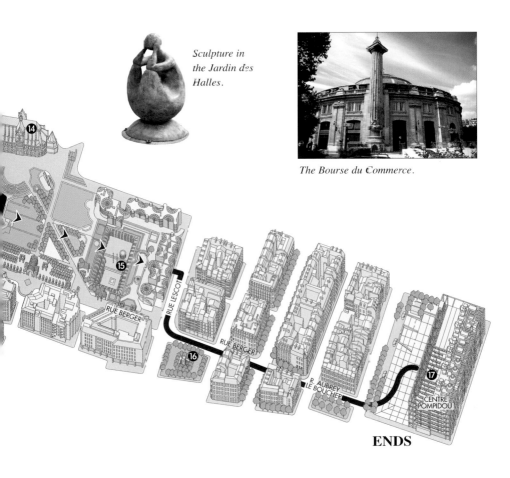

Sculpture in the Jardin des Halles.

The Bourse du Commerce.

ENDS

16 You will surface, finally, in a ticky-tacky pedestrian zone, passing on your way one pleasurable sight: the charming Renaissance **Fontaine des Innocents,** whose little square has become a resting place for weary backpackers and an obstacle course for skateboarders.

17 Despite its surreal modernity (it caused a sensation when it opened in 1977) the **Pompidou Centre** has already required extensive renovation and refurbishment. Now is a great

Fontaine des Innocents.

time to visit – before the paint starts peeling again on all those exterior escalators, lifts and ducts. The **Musée National d'Art Moderne** is a must, with a stunning collection of early 20thC art on Level 5, including works by Picasso, Braque, Matisse and Miró. There are also temporary exhibitions, a cinema, an important multimedia library, a music 'laboratory' and, on the top floor, a sleek restaurant/café with more fabulous views over Paris.

103

Nobility Regained: The Marais

Relais St Gervais

Street sign, rue François-Miron.

This fascinating and distinctly different district rose from marshland (*marais*) in the 17th century to become crammed with beautiful mansions occupied by royalty and nobility. Its demise during the Revolution was inevitable and swift, and it wasn't until the 1960s that attention again turned to ruined pre-Revolutionary architecture and restoration began. Today it is buzzing; several of its *hôtels* have become prestigious museums, and a young crowd hang out in the cafés and browse in the fashion shops.

The route passes the principal landmarks in the Marais, but it is not one which you need to slavishly follow: it's a great place for simply following your nose and seeing where you end up. It's a walk on which you should push open doors and sneak into courtyards, and watch out for street signs, stone plaques and ornate portals. Try to avoid weekends, when the place is packed.

▶ **STARTS**
Rue de Rivoli, at junction with rue François-Miron.
Nearest metro: St Paul.

■ **ENDS**
Place des Vosges.
Nearest metro: St Paul, Bastille.

RUE DE BRAQUE

RUE RAMBUTEAU

R. DES ARCHIVES

R. STE CROIX DE LA BRETONNERIE

R. DE LA VERRERIE

RUE DE RIVOLI

R. DE LOBAU

PL. ST GERVAIS

QUAI DE L'HOTEL DE VILLE

R. DES BARRES

R. DU PONT LOUIS-PHILIPPE

R. GRENIER-SUR-L'EAU

R. GEOFFROY L'ASNIER

QUAI DE L'HOTEL DE VILLE

R. DE L'HOTEL-DE-VILLE

VOIE GEORGES POMPIDOU

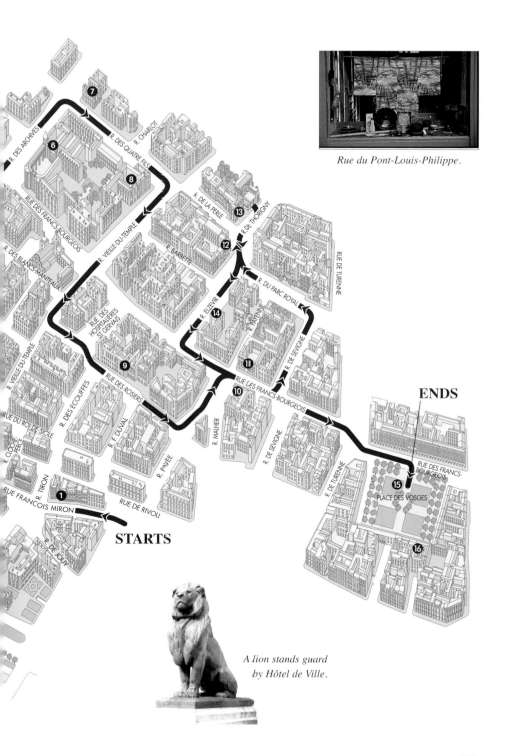

Rue du Pont-Louis-Philippe.

ENDS

STARTS

*A lion stands guard
by Hôtel de Ville.*

105

❶ Rue François-Miron has several fine old buildings. No. 68, Hôtel de Beauvais, is one of the last great Marais mansions to be renovated: try hard and you might glimpse its magnificent courtyard. It was built for Anne of Austria's lady-in-waiting and confidante Catherine Bellier, who had earned the queen's gratitude by proving, beyond all doubt, that the young Louis XIV did not share his father's frequent impotence. At **Nos 44-46,** the Maison d'Ourscamp, with a fine Gothic cellar, houses an association dedicated to saving Paris's historic buildings. The sudden appearance of two narrow, crooked half-timbered houses announces **Nos 11 and 13,** rare medieval buildings.

Medieval houses, rue François-Miron.

❷ Turn left down smart **rue du Pont-Louis-Philippe** – with its elegant, expensive shops and a sudden view of the Panthéon in the distance – to explore an attractive group of streets close to the Seine. At Alleé des Justes turn left (look to the right for a charming view), passing a silver **Wallace Fountain** (see page 31), which originally had little cups attached by metal chains. Turn right into rue Geoffroy l'Asnier to see the **Mémorial du Martyr Juif Inconnu,** erected in 1956, with an eternal flame burning in its crypt, commemorating the victims of the Holocaust. Notice, across the road, the

At the Mémorial du Martyr Juif Inconnu.

fine portal of **Hôtel Chalons de Luxembourg.** There are several restaurants: for a budget meal, try timeless **Le Trumilou** (84 quai de l'Hôtel de Ville; tel. 01 42 77 63 98); or take the window table for two at **Chez Julien** (1 rue du Pont-Louis-Philippe; tel. 01 42 78 31 64).

❸ Climb the shallow steps, sprinkled with café tables and chairs, up pretty **rue des Barres.** Pass under the flying gargoyles at the back of the church of St-Gervais-St-Protais, and noting **No. 12,** what must be the most attractive youth hostel in France.

Chez Julien.

❹ You can enter **St-Gervais-St-Protais,** built on a mound which once rose above the marshland, by the rear door in rue des Barres. This soaring church has great serenity, engendered in part by the Fraternity of Jerusalem, an order of urban nuns and monks who work part-time and worship with their congregation, not separately. The church's fine organ was played by François Couperin and his family for generations. Leave by the front entrance, turning round to see the church's superb classical façade.

Charming Rue des Barres.

5 In workaday **rue des Archives,** Paris' only surviving medieval cloisters can be seen at **Eglise des Billettes;** temporary art exhibitions are held there. Further along, **Maison Coeur,** now a school, was the medieval home of financier-diplomat Jacques Coeur.

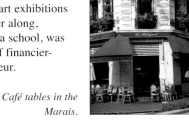

Hôtel Chalons de Luxembourg.

Café tables in the Marais.

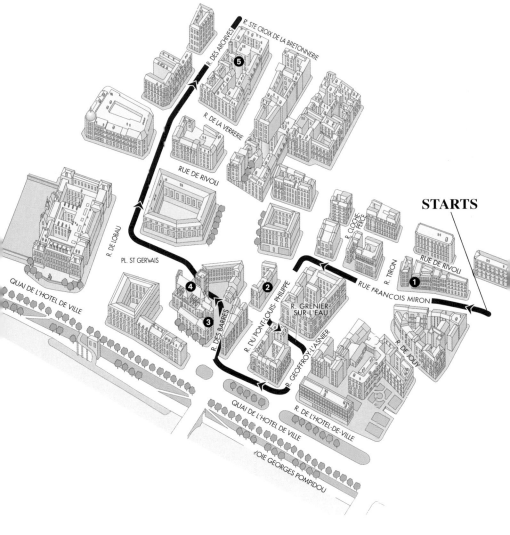

107

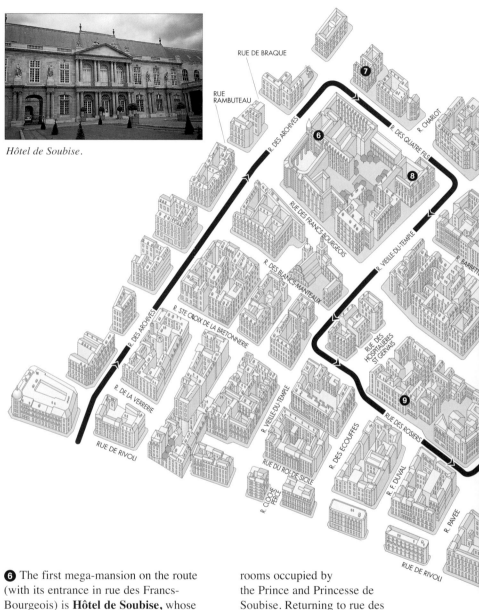

Hôtel de Soubise.

6 The first mega-mansion on the route (with its entrance in rue des Francs-Bourgeois) is **Hôtel de Soubise,** whose splendour makes one realize just how rarefied the Marais was before the French Revolution. It houses the **Archives Nationales** and the **Musée de l'Histoire de France** (open 2pm-5pm, closed Tues), worth visiting for the opportunity to see the rococo rooms occupied by the Prince and Princesse de Soubise. Returning to rue des Archives, notice the **Gothic turreted gate,** all that survives of the 14thC manor house of a famous knight, Olivier de Clisson. On the corner of rue des Haudriettes is the 18thC **Fontaine des Haudriettes,** adorned with a lovely sleeping maid.

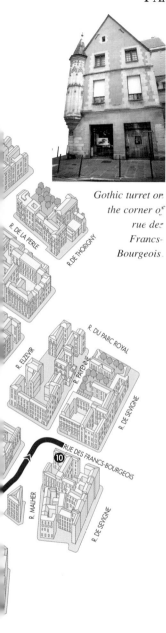

Gothic turret on the corner of rue des Francs-Bourgeois

❼ In the perfectly proportioned **Hôtel Guénégaud** (by François Marsart) is the **Musée de la Chasse et de la Nature.** Frankly you have to be an enthusiast for guns, antlers, mounted heads and stuffed animals and classical hunting paintings to fully appreciate this place. In one room, dozens of stuffed animals – gorillas, tigers, panthers and a tiny Kirk's dik dik – stand in mid-roar. (Closed Mon.)

❽ **Hôtel de Rohan** (which also houses the **Archives Nationales**) has an inviting garden that can be glimpsed through its tall, elegant windows. Cross rue des Francs-Bourgeois (note the surviving **Gothic turret** on the corner), continue to rue des Rosiers and turn left, unless you want to pause for refuelling a few paces on down rue Vieille-du-Temple. Choose from: trendy **Les Philosophes** (No. 28, open until 2 am) which hosts philosophy breakfasts on Sunday mornings; **Au Petit Fer à Cheval** (No. 30), with its original horseshoe-shaped bar, ceramic tiles and mirrors; or **La Belle Hortense** (No. 31), a wine bar and bookshop which also hosts art exhibitions. Cul-de-sac **rue de Trésor** was so named because in 1882, during a demolition here, a copper vase filled with 14thC gold coins was unearthed.

❾ Narrow **rue des Rosiers** is the backbone of the city's Jewish quarter, first settled in the 13th century. It has an atmosphere all its own, far removed from the patrician mansions that surround it. A highlight is the delicatessen **Sacha Finkelsztajn.** Go here for the musicians, the eclectic mix of customers, the comic English translations on the menu and the equally comic surliness of the waiters. The street also houses several kosher *boulangeries,* one of which is in a lovely old 19th century shop (**No. 16**).

❿ Drop into the fine reading room of the **Bibliothèque Historique de la Ville de Paris** in Hôtel de Lamoignon. Look at the pediment above the tall Corinthian columns of the façade: its hunting symbols recall Diana, goddess of hunting because the *hôtel* was built for another Diana, daughter of Henri II. This street, **rue Pavée,** is so named because it was one of the first to be paved in Paris.

⓫ Now comes a clutch of museums, so you must decide which ones to give your time to. Emerging in rue des Francs-Bourgeois, peer through iron mesh to see the lovely green courtyard of **Hôtel de Carnavalet,** which houses the **Musée Carnavalet,** tracing the history of Paris. It was the home, from 1677-96, of Madame de Sévigné. Her sparkling correspondence makes an invaluable record of her life in the Marais, where she lived in no less than nine properties. (Closed Mon.)

⓬ Another beautiful mansion, **Hôtel Libéral-Bruand,** designed for himself by the eponymous architect of the Invalides, houses the **Musée de la Serrure.** Its stone-vaulted cellars make a refreshingly quiet and cool place in which to admire the art of the locksmith over the centuries. (Closed Sat, Sun.)

Musée Picasso.

Place des Vosges.

⓭ An unmissable highlight, not just of the Marais but of all Paris, is the **Musée Picasso** in **Hôtel Salé,** a highly complementary marriage between the modernity of Picasso's art and the calm graciousness of this 17thC mansion. The collection, left to the French government (in lieu of taxes) after Picasso's death, spans the whole of his long and creative life. (Closed Tues.)

⓮ For a complete contrast, take a quick look round **Hôtel Donon,** stuffed to the gills with the frothy 18thC contents – paintings, porcelain, furniture, *objets d'art* – of the **Musée Cognacq-Jay.** The founders of the Samaritaine department store, Ernest Cognacq and his wife Louise Jay, left this collection to the nation in the 1920s. There is much to admire here, including a tiny, idealized portrait of beautiful *Mr Hope* by Henry Bone; a little portrait of Madame de Pompadour's daughter by Drouais; and the charming, intimate *Le Doux Réveil* by Boilly. (Closed Mon.)

⓯ It's not just the perfect symmetry of place des Vosges (the oldest square in Paris), but the mellow colours of its brick, stone and slate that make it so magical. Unfortunately its central garden is rarely very peaceful these days. Take refuge instead at **Ma Bourgogne** (tel. 01 42 78 44 64) or in the romantically situated **Hotel Pavilion de la Reine** on the north side.

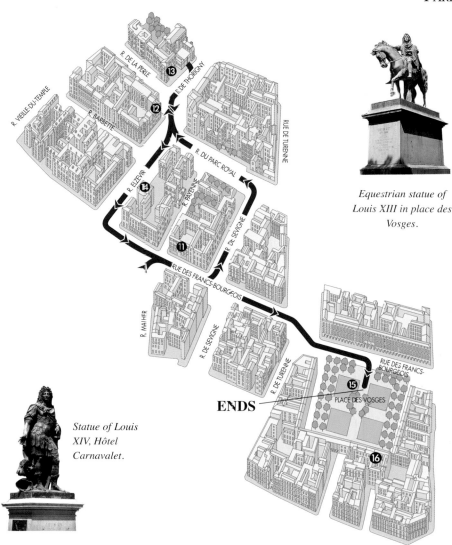

Equestrian statue of
Louis XIII in place des
Vosges.

ENDS

Statue of Louis
XIV, Hôtel
Carnavalet.

16 To best appreciate the harmony of **place des Vosges,** you
should proceed to the second floor apartment in **Maison de
Victor Hugo,** where the splendid view is unobscured by
trees. This was the home of the novelist and dramatist from
1832-1848, becoming a museum in 1903 on the instigation
of his friend and admirer Paul Meurice, who donated much
of the memorabilia and the dire, specially commissioned
paintings. Despite its creaky floorboards and a faint smell of
mothballs, the museum is worth visiting for the
reconstruction of the Salon Chinoise, a room Hugo created
at the Guernsey home of his mistress, Juliette Drouet, just a
few paces from his own house (Closed Mon.)

Storming the Galleries: Village St Paul and Bastille

From the charming courtyards, ancient buildings, elegant churches and bustling high street that characterize the edge of the Marais, this walk plunges – via the Arsenal – into the Bastille. This traditionally working-class neighbourhood has undergone a comprehensive rejuvenation programme with the arrival of the Bastille Opéra and a host of trendy new galleries, shops, restaurants and bars. The area has been dubbed the 'SoHo of Paris'. Its gentrification continues but elements of the area's modest roots are still in evidence. On rue Faubourg St Antoine, for example, craftsmen's workshops are sandwiched between minimalist bars and fashionable shops. In the 17th century, Faubourg St Antoine was the hub of manufacturing in Paris because Louis XIV attracted members of artisan and craft guilds to the district by exempting them from paying taxes. Many members of these guilds were among the revolutionaries who fought for freedom and stormed the Bastille. Emigré tradesmen from the Auvergne moved into the area in the early 20th century, to be followed by struggling artists. As the area is smartened up and rents rocket, it is these very people who can no longer afford to stay.

Hôtel de Sully.

ENDS

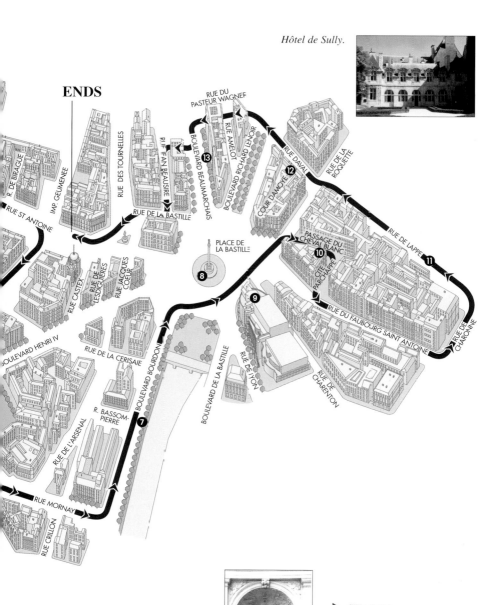

Fountain in rue Charlemagne.

▶ **STARTS**
Rue de Rivoli. Nearest
metro: St Paul.

■ **ENDS**
Place de la Bastille. Nearest
metro: Bastille.

113

Hôtel de Sens.

❶ Rounding the curve in rue du Figuier, the pale stonework and slate-roofed pepperpot turrets of the **Hôtel de Sens** rise into view. It looks like the set for an Errol Flynn film, but is in fact a perfect medieval residence. Built in the 14th century, it was remodelled between 1475 and 1507 by Tristan de Salazar, Archbishop of Sens, who tried to create the illusion of a fortified castle by adding Gothic touches such as a dungeon and watchtower. Up on the eastern façade you can see a hole made in 1830 by a stray cannonball, embedded in the stone to this day. The grand structure now houses the **Forney Library,** specializing in fine arts. (Tues-Sat 1.30pm-7pm.)

❷ Rue des Jardins St Paul skirts a school playground, enclosed on the far side by a 228-foot (70m) stretch of **ancient wall,** the most substantial relic of Philip Augustus' 1190 fortifications. At Nos 10-14, turn into **Village St Paul,** a series of interconnecting cobbled courtyards surrounded by a charming huddle of workshops, galleries, antique and craft shops. Dolls' clothes, bric-à-brac, furniture and paintings are often displayed outside and the courtyards have all the lively atmosphere of a street market. (Closed Tues, Wed.)

Bric-`a-brac for sale in Village St-Paul.

❸ Walk past the pretty fountain (1840) in rue Charlemagne at the back of the church of St Paul-St Louis and into the little passage, **rue Eginhard,** a Jewish enclave from the 17th century. A monument in the garden on the left pays moving tribute to a father and his three sons who died in Auschwitz. Restaurants and antique shops jostle for space in **rue St Paul.** If you need sustenance, try **L'Enoteca** (25 rue Charles-V; tel. 01 42 78 91 44), a good-value Italian trattoria; or **Le Rouge-Gorge** (8 rue St Paul; tel. 01 48 04 75 89), an engaging old café/bar (off map).

STARTS

❹ The narrow, cobbled passage de St-Paul leads to the Jesuit church of **St Paul-St Louis,** modelled on the Gesù in Rome and Madame de Sévigné's chosen place of worship. It lost most of its treasures during the Revolution, but one masterpiece remains: *Christ in the Garden,* a rare religious painting by Delacroix. Leave by the main door and turn onto **rue St Antoine,** a busy down-to-earth shopping street. At No. 62 is the elegant late-Renaissance **Hôtel de Sully** by Jean Androuet de Cerceau, who also built the lovely **Hôtel de Mayenne** at Nos 21-23.

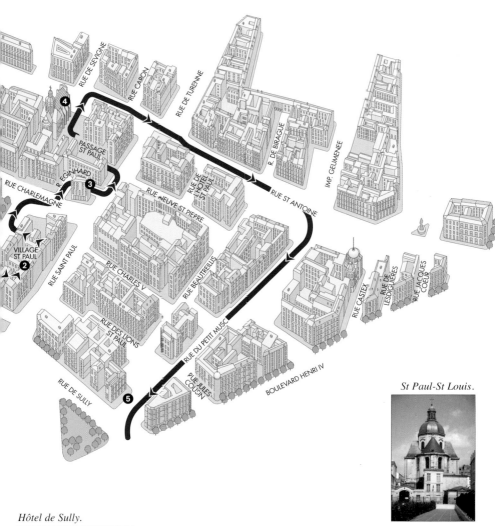

St Paul-St Louis.

Hôtel de Sully.

5 On the *quai* at the end of rue du Petit Music, a calm street away from the hurly-burly, stands the late-16thC **Hôtel Fieubet** with its extravagant 19thC façade of faux-baroque mouldings. The mansion was a gift to Gaspard Fieubet, Queen Marie-Thérèse's Chancellor, who employed Jules Hardouin-Mansart as interior decorator. It is now a school and sadly dilapidated. Opposite is **square Henri Galli,** an oasis of calm amid thundering traffic, where you can see chunks of the Bastille prison, found in rue St Antoine while excavating the metro.

❻ A fascinating exhibition on the evolution and architecture of Paris is contained in the **Pavillon d'Arsenal,** a late-19thC warehouse with a stone façade and glass roof. The display spans the centuries from Philip Augustus to Métro 2000 via Haussmann. In a pretty sandstone house opposite, built in 1594 for Henri IV's Grand Master of Artillery, is the **Bibliothèque de l'Arsenal.** At the top of a grand staircase lined with bronze and marble busts, you can visit reading rooms with moulded ceilings, stacks filled with leather-bound tomes (many concerned with theatre), a collection of illuminated manuscripts, and the Bastille archives including the death certificate of the 'man in the iron mask'. To see the apartments (the music room is a gem), contact the Caisse Nationale des Monuments Historiques (tel. 01 44 61 21 50), which organizes group tours. (Closed Sun.)

L'homme aux semelles devant, opposite the Bibliothèque de l'Arsenal.

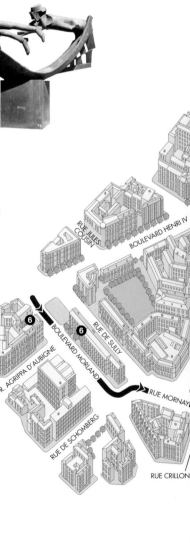

❼ When you reach **Port de Plaisance de l'Arsenal,** cross over the footbridge to the boulevard de la Bastille side (off map). Here the cobbled *quai* is bordered by a grassy bank, a perfect picnic spot. Part of the 19th century industrial Canal St Martin, built for the Faubourg St Antoine manufacturers, the waterway enjoys life today as a marina, where colourful barges jostle with gin palaces.

Boat on the Canal St Martin.

❽ Where the city's notorious prison-fortress stood from 1370 to 1789, traffic now roars around the hectic junction of **place de la Bastille.** The prison, reserved for VIPs who had fallen foul of the king, was famously stormed by revolutionaries on 14 July 1789, an event celebrated with national gusto ever since. The only physical reminder is an outline of the building on the pavement. The **Colonne de Juillet,** a verdigris-bronze column topped by a gilded *génie* of liberty, commemorates those who died in the three-day revolution of July 1830. The remains of hundreds of victims of the two uprisings are contained in its crypt, which you can enter through the plinth.

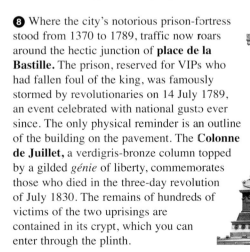

Colonne de Juillet, place de la Bastille.

Opéra Bastille.

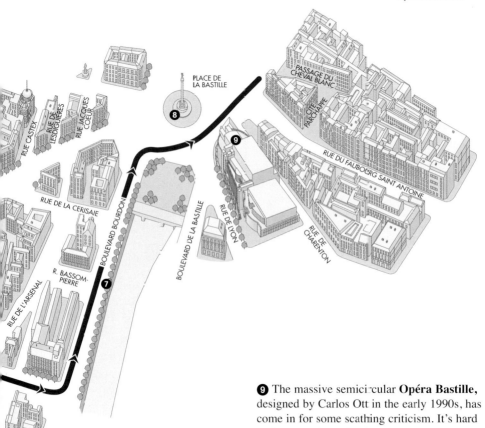

*Port de
Plaisance,
Canal St
Martin.*

9 The massive semicircular **Opéra Bastille,**
designed by Carlos Ott in the early 1990s, has
come in for some scathing criticism. It's hard
to deny that its white tiled exterior suggests an
immense public lavatory. However, it now
stages most of the city's opera and, in
introducing culture to the district, has been
crucial in transforming the Bastille from a run-
down ghetto into one of the capital's grooviest
neighbourhoods. Next door, a 17thC tavern has
developed into a huge brasserie, **Les Grandes
Marches,** popular with tourists and the post-
opera crowd (tel. 01 43 42 90 32).

❿ From place de la Bastille, turn into **passage du Cheval Blanc,** one of a clutch of cobbled alleyways off rue Faubourg St Antoine. Leading off from the passage are several courtyards named after months of the year, and these house some of the remaining workshops of cabinet-makers and craftsmen, whose shops you will find on bustling **rue Faubourg St Antoine** (evidence of this street's long association with crafts). Stop for a drink or lunch at one of the trendy bar/restaurants that have moved in with the gentrification of the area, like **La Fabrique** at No. 51.

You could extend the walk by continuing along rue du Faubourg St Antoine until you reach **rue d'Aligre** (off map) on your right, where market stalls run the long length of the street and into place d'Aligre. As well as fruit and vegetables, traders here hawk North African produce, spices, meat, cheese, bric-à-brac and clothing. More permanent stalls in the **Beauveau St Antoine,** a covered market built in 1843, sell more of the same. (Closed pm.)

⓫ The duality of the area hits you as you turn into **rue de Lappe,** where chic boutiques and galleries exist cheek by jowl with traditional restaurants and ateliers. Named after Girard de Lappe, whose 17thC garden it carved up, the road became an Auvergnat stronghold. Harking back to that time, **La Galoche d'Aurillac** is a gloriously old-fashioned restaurant, its ceiling appropriately decorated with rows of clogs (No. 41; tel. 01 47 00 77 15). At No. 6, **Chez Teil** sells cheese, paté, salamis – crowded on hooks in the window – and other products from the Auvergne. It was in this road that the *bal musette* (dance hall) took off. At one time there were 15. Now only **Le Balajo** at No. 9 remains: a one-time haunt of Edith Piaf, now a 21stC disco.

⓬ As you walk down rue Daval, pop into picture-perfect **cour Damoye,** an alley used in so many movies that it's difficult to know which shopfronts are genuine and which are fake. Continue until you reach **boulevard Richard Lenoir,** built by Haussmann over the Canal St Martin, where a no-frills (some would say tacky) morning street market gives a taste of what life in the area used to be like. Stalls here sell a range of products from fruit and veg to linen and soap; it's livelier on Sundays.

Tiled decoration on 28 boulevard Beaumarchais.

⓭ At **2-20 boulevard Beaumarchais** there is no sign of the sumptuous house and grounds owned by the 18thC dramatist and librettist Caron de Beaumarchais, which stood on this spot. However, you can see his statue, cane tucked under arm, at the end of the walk on the corner of rues des Tournelles and St Antoine. From boulevard Beaumarchais, thread your way through the narrow streets until you reach rue de la Bastille. At No. 5, **Bofinger** (tel. 01 42 72 05 23) is a traditional brasserie that has been in business since 1864. Decorated in exuberant Art Nouveau style, it now attracts more tourists than locals.

Statue of Caron de Beaumarchais.

Tapas Nocturne in rue de Lappe.

Shop sign in cour Damoye.

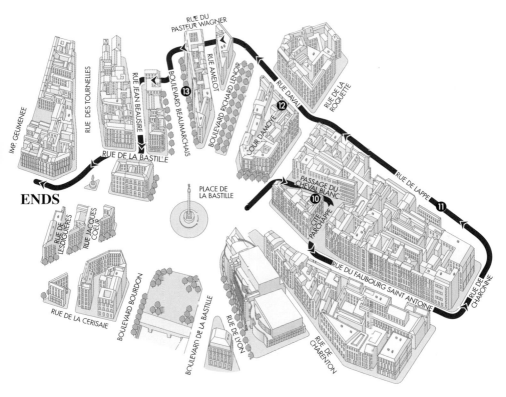

Island Hopping: Ile St Louis and Ile de la Cité

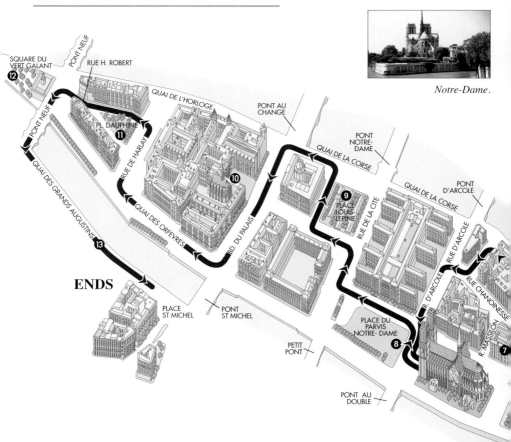

Notre-Dame.

► STARTS
Boulevard Henri IV. Nearest
metro: Sully Morland.

■ ENDS
Quai des Grands Augustins.
Nearest metro: St Michel.

Paris began on the Ile de la Cité.
When the Romans arrived in 53BC, they
found a primitive Celtic settlement here called
Lutetia. The island was settled again in the 3rd
century by the Parisii tribe who gave the city its
name. By the Middle Ages it was a centre of
power – political, ecclesiastical and legal – borne
out by the Gothic *tour de force*, Notre-Dame, and
the gem of Ste Chapelle. Although the island did
not escape Baron Haussmann's sweeping 19thC
changes, which destroyed its huddle of medieval
streets, this walk takes you to some charming
hidden corners, such as rue Chanoinesse, place

Pleasure boat on the Seine.

Dauphine and square du Vert-Galant. The walk begins on the Ile St Louis, a more private and picturesque island that seems to tag along behind its larger neighbour. Named after Louis IX, it is an architectural feast, its fine mansions, *hôtels particuliers*, all built together in the 17th century. The Ile St Louis is made for walking, whether down its bustling little main street or along its quiet, beautifully preserved *quais*. Try to do this walk on a Sunday (Apr-Nov) when both Left and Right Bank *quais* are closed to traffic.

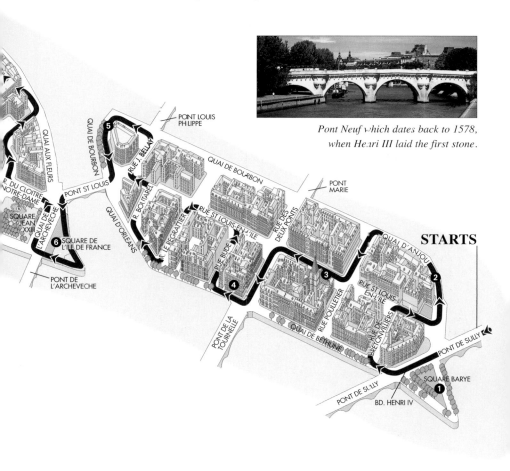

Pont Neuf which dates back to 1578, when Henri III laid the first stone.

① When you step onto the island, take a moment to admire its main street. Rue St Louis-en-l'Ile runs in a straight line from one end to the other, allowing you to see the island's entire narrow, alluring length. Lavishly planted with trees, flowers and shrubs, **square Barye** is the last vestige of the glorious terraced gardens of the Hôtel de Bretonvilliers, which stood on the charming cobbled **quai de Béthune**. With its decorations by Poussin and its unrivalled location, the mansion's magnificence put its grand neighbours in the shade. All that remains today is its 'back door', a quirky pavilion perched improbably above the arch over the end of **rue Bretonvilliers.**

Stained glass in St Louis-en-l'Ile.

② As soon as you turn into **quai d'Anjou,** you will see why it has always appealed to artists. Tranquil beside the river, its *hôtels* form a string of architectural pearls – many untouched – designed by Louis XIV's architect, Louis Le Vau. **Hôtel Lambert** at No.1 was built in 1640 for Lambert the Rich, with a sumptuous interior by Charles Le Brun, the man responsible for the Hall of Mirrors at Versailles. A romantic roof garden, enclosed by an elaborate wrought-iron balcony, tops its unusual circular turret. Le Vau and Le Brun also collaborated on the splendid **Hôtel de Lausun** (No. 17) in 1657. In the 19th century, Baudelaire and Gautier both rented apartments here, and it became the headquarters of the Hashish-Eaters' Club. Plaques on the mansion walls bear witness to the status of former residents.

③ A favourite for society weddings, the baroque church of **St Louis-en-l'Ile** was built between 1664 and 1726 according to plans by Le Vau. The exterior is distinguished by its curious pierced spire. The interior, despite a ransacking during the Revolution, is a riot of marble and gold, a romantic venue for the candlelit concerts staged here.

Outside, **rue St Louis-en-l'Ile** is the spine of the island, busy with local people doing their day-to-day shopping as well as tourists drawn to the chic galleries, bookshops, delicatessens, restaurants and a clutch of charming hotels. The most stylish of these is the **Hôtel du Jeu de Paume** at No. 54, an innovative conversion of a 17thC tennis court. At No. 31 is the original **Berthillon,** maker of the city's most delicious ice cream. It has become so popular in recent years that queues often stretch for a couple of blocks despite two newer branches on the island.

Window of Galerie Jacqueline Lemoine formerly in rue St-Louis-en-l'Ile.

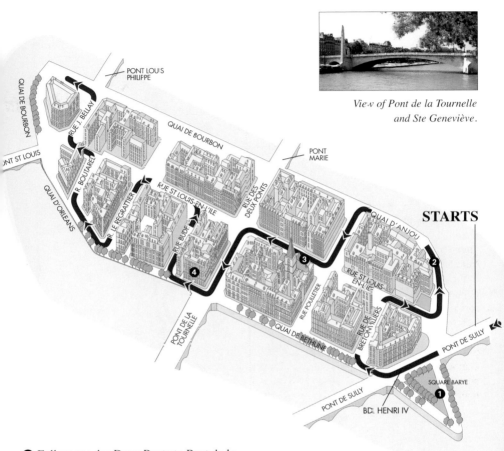

View of Pont de la Tournelle and Ste Geneviève.

❹ Follow rue des Deux Ponts to Pont de la Tournelle, and look across the river to the flower-decked barges and the cloaked statue of Ste Geneviève, patron saint of Paris. To your right, **quai d'Orléans** has many fine *hôtels*, including No. 6, where expatriate Poles used to meet in the 19th century. It is now **Musée Adam Mickiewicz,** named after the 19thC romantic emigré poet who amassed an extensive library and the largest collection of Polish writing, art and memorabilia outside Poland – including Chopin's death mask. (Open Sat am, Thurs pm.)

Quai d'Orléans.

❺ If you lunch at the brash Alsatian **Brasserie de l'Ile St Louis** (tel. 01 43 54 02 59), which spreads over the corner of rues Jean du Bellay and St Louis-en-l'Ile, instead of pudding you might buy an ice cream from Berthillon on quai d'Orléans. Stroll past **41-53 quai de Bourbon,** the handsome *hôtels* built by François Le Vau (brother of Louis), and rest on one of the benches at the lovely, shady tip of the island. This is a popular lovers' trysting-place with a glorious view of the Ile de la Cité, (the next leg of your walk).

❻ Cross pedestrian **Pont St Louis,** an impromptu stage for street performers, and head for the well-tended square de l'Ile de France, where you can descend into the **Mémorial des Martyrs et de la Déportation.** The stark modern design of this harrowing memorial to the 200,000 French deportees and victims of the holocaust combines concrete and black grilles, hemming you in physically and symbolically. Across the street, **square Jean XXIII,** on the site of the archbishop's palace, is filled with trees and flowers around a 19thC Gothic fountain. The park affords a terrific view of the flying buttresses that soar up the eastern end of Notre-Dame.

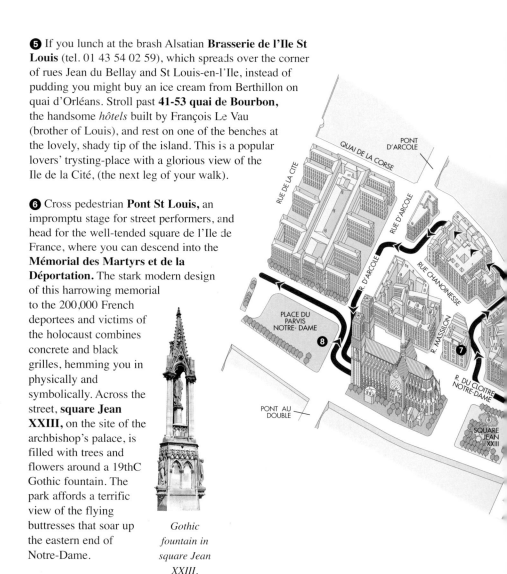

Gothic fountain in square Jean XXIII.

❼ Before you turn off rue du Cloître-Notre-Dame, try to visit the tiny **Musée de Notre-Dame de Paris,** hidden away further down the street at No. 10. Overlooked by most tourists, it is crammed with fascinating artifacts including a 17thC faience pot and two decorative bronze bees created for Napoleon's investiture, as well as documents, engravings, paintings and photographs. (Open Wed, Sat, Sun 2.30-6pm.) A plaque on **9 quai aux Fleurs** marks the spot where star-crossed lovers Abelard and Héloïse lived.

Right: Notre-Dame.
Below: the West Rose window.

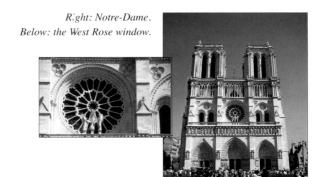

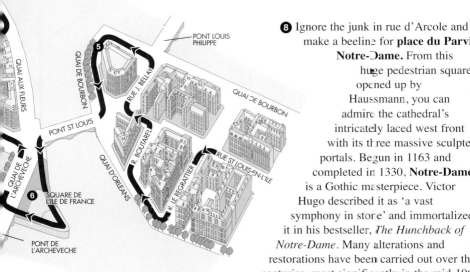

❽ Ignore the junk in rue d'Arcole and make a beeline for **place du Parvis Notre-Dame.** From this huge pedestrian square, opened up by Haussmann, you can admire the cathedral's intricately laced west front with its three massive sculpted portals. Begun in 1163 and completed in 1330, **Notre-Dame** is a Gothic masterpiece. Victor Hugo described it as 'a vast symphony in stone' and immortalized it in his bestseller, *The Hunchback of Notre-Dame.* Many alterations and restorations have been carried out over the centuries, most significantly in the mid-19th century by Viollet-le-Duc, who built the cathedral's distinctive spire. If you have the energy – and if the queue is not too long – climb one of the towers for the panorama of the city and a close-up of the fabulous gargoyles and griffins.

Back in the square, don't miss the **Crypte Archéologique** in the south-western corner, where 3rdC Gallo-Roman ramparts and medieval remains (unearthed during excavations) are superbly displayed (Closed Mon). On the north side, **Hôtel Dieu,**

Haussmann's Hôtel Dieu.

porates a quirky little hotel, Hospitel.

125

9 From Monday to Saturday **place Louis-Lépine** is awash with the colour and fragrance of the city's principal flower market; on Sunday, when caged birds replace the flowers, it's alive with birdsong. On the south side of the square is a rare survivor: one of Hector Guimard's curvaceous Art Nouveau metro entrances.

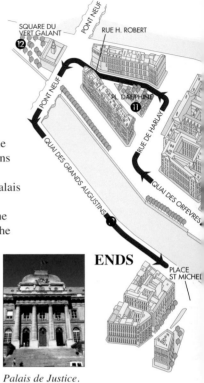

Gates to the Palais de Justice from the boulevard du Palais.

10 Through the imposing gateway on boulevard du Palais, enter the complex of buildings that runs the width of the island and contains the Conciergerie, Palais de Justice and Ste Chapelle. Antechamber to the guillotine during the Reign of Terror, the **Conciergerie** is where Marie Antoinette was kept in a dank cell. Ironically it is now the setting for concerts, plays and wine tastings – usually held in the magnificent Salle des Gens d'Armes. The splendid 14th century kitchen also survives, with four fireplaces each large enough to roast a whole ox, as well as the 13thC Tour Bonbec torture chamber.

On the site of a Roman palace and France's first royal residence (which later became the 14thC seat of parliament), the **Palais de Justice** is now home to the law courts. Mainly rebuilt in the 19thC after two fires, its most impressive rooms are the 13thC Salle de Pas-Perdus and the blue-and-gold Première Chambre, where Marie Antoinette was condemned. (Closed Sat, Sun.)

The highlight of the complex is the two-tiered **Ste Chapelle,** built by Louis IX in the 1240s to house relics. A spiral staircase leads from the lower chapel to a soaring upper chapel into which jewel-toned light streams through vast stained-glass windows. The upper chapel has marvellous acoustics and concerts are staged here most evenings.

Palais de Justice.

Statue of Henri IV in place du Pont Neuf.

11 Quai des Orfèvres, once the province of goldsmiths (and now the police), leads to **place Dauphine,** a peaceful triangular square designed by Henri IV and named for his son (the future Louis XIII). It is lined with charming 17thC houses, some stone, others brick: many now occupied by restaurants such as the archetypal bistro, **Paul** (No. 15; tel. 01 43 54 21 48); and **Le Caveau du Palais** (No. 19; tel 01 43 26 04 28), with an imaginative menu and a cosy atmosphere.

*Fountain in place
Louis-Lépine.*

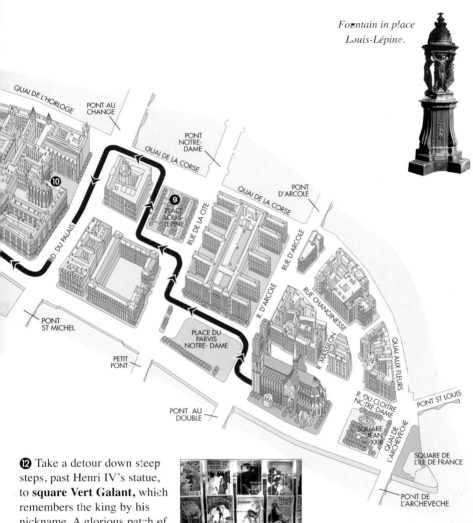

⑫ Take a detour down steep steps, past Henri IV's statue, to **square Vert Galant,** which remembers the king by his nickname. A glorious patch of grass enclosed by shady walks and flower beds, this is the point from which the Vedettes du Pont Neuf (pleasure boats) leave on their hour-long cruises (departures every 30 mins). Taking one might be an excellent way to end your walk. Alternatively, retrace your steps and leave the island via **Pont Neuf,** which, despite its name, was completed in 1607 and is the oldest bridge in Paris.

*Bouquiniste's display on
quai des Grands
Augustins.*

⑬ Finally, stroll along **quai des Grands Augustins,** pausing to browse at the many *bouquinistes,* the famous Left Bank stalls selling second-hand books, prints, maps and posters. If you need to revive yourself, there's a splendid choice of wines and cheeses at the delightful Art Deco **Bistro des Augustins** (No. 39; tel. 01 43 54 45 75).

127

Leonie Glass is a travel writer and editor. She edited several major books at Mitchell Beazley and is co-editor of Duncan Petersen's *Charming Small Hotel Guides* (see www.charmingsmallhotels.co.uk).

Fiona Duncan writes a weekly column for the *Sunday Telegraph* called the Hotel Guru (see www.thehotelguru.com).